WEDGWOOD

Color Plate I, No. 346. Vase and cover, cane ware, imitation bamboo, painted design, Etruria 1790. Height 9″.

WEDGWOOD

BY JOHN MEREDITH GRAHAM II AND

HENSLEIGH CECIL WEDGWOOD

THE BROOKLYN MUSEUM

THE BROOKLYN INSTITUTE OF ARTS AND SCIENCES

COVER: *The figures are drawn after the plaque, "Dancing Hours," by John Flaxman.*

PRINTED IN THE UNITED STATES OF AMERICA BY
THE JOHN B. WATKINS COMPANY, NEW YORK, N. Y.
EDITION: 20,000.

FOREWORD

The Brooklyn Museum is glad of the opportunity to present to the public the exhibition, "Wedgwood — A Living Tradition." Here will be found a detailed and documented visual history of the accomplishments of ten generations of a single family, whose name has become a household word. The work of this single family is consistently distinguished by its excellence, and it can fairly be said to represent a typical cross section of more than three hundred years of the history of the whole English ceramic industry. For Gilbert Wedgwood, first known potter of the family, employed in 1612 only the crudest of handicraft methods, while the Wedgwood industry of today incorporates in its modern plant the latest developments in the science of manufacture and of industrial relations. Between these two extremes is shown the contribution in taste and technique which each age made to the sum total which the name "Wedgwood" conveys to us today.

Special emphasis is naturally placed on the great period from 1759-1795 during which Josiah Wedgwood was making his forward strides in ceramic art. For Josiah was a pioneer not alone as a potter in his own right, but as one who believed that only the best was good enough to be associated with his name: the best artists, the most up-to-date mechanical improvements, the most painstaking experimentation, and the most enlightened concern for the well-being of his employees.

In an address upon the opening of the Wedgwood Museum in 1863 the Right Honorable W. E. Gladstone said "Josiah Wedgwood was the greatest man who ever, in any age or any country, applied himself to the important work of uniting art with industry." It is from the collections of this Museum that many unique treasures, which have never before left England, have graciously been permitted to come to this country.

Mr. Hensleigh Wedgwood has not only been tireless in his efforts to make the exhibition possible, but has made important contributions from his special knowledge of the history of Wedgwood to the text of this handbook. To Miss Annie Reese of the Wedgwood organization thanks are due for her helpful cooperation in organizing the show from its inception and especially for her preparatory work in connection with this handbook.

We are indebted to Josiah Wedgwood and Sons, Inc., of America for their enterprise and generosity in arranging for the loan of material belonging to the parent company and members of the Wedgwood family. To those institutions which have lent from their collections or which have aided us in bringing the story of Wedgwood to a larger segment of the American public by circulating the exhibition our thanks are due. Credit for the designing and installation of the exhibit should go to Mr. John Meredith Graham II, Curator of the Department of Decorative Arts, and for photographs to Mr. Anthony Caruso, museum photographer.

CHARLES NAGEL, JR.
Director

CONTENTS

THE WEDGWOOD FAMILY

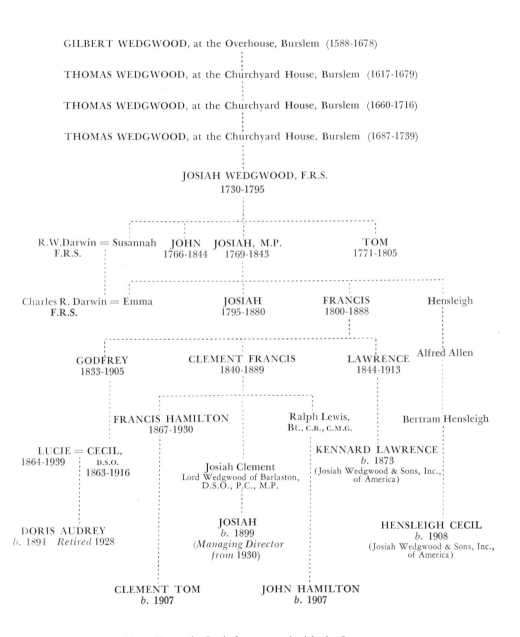

GILBERT WEDGWOOD, at the Overhouse, Burslem (1588-1678)

THOMAS WEDGWOOD, at the Churchyard House, Burslem (1617-1679)

THOMAS WEDGWOOD, at the Churchyard House, Burslem (1660-1716)

THOMAS WEDGWOOD, at the Churchyard House, Burslem (1687-1739)

JOSIAH WEDGWOOD, F.R.S.
1730-1795

R.W.Darwin = Susannah   JOHN   JOSIAH, M.P.   TOM
F.R.S.   1766-1844 1769-1843   1771-1805

Charles R. Darwin = Emma   JOSIAH   FRANCIS   Hensleigh
F.R.S.   1795-1880   1800-1888

GODFREY   CLEMENT FRANCIS   LAWRENCE   Alfred Allen
1833-1905   1840-1889   1844-1913

FRANCIS HAMILTON   Ralph Lewis,   Bertram Hensleigh
1867-1930   Bt., C.B., C.M.G.

LUCIE = CECIL,   KENNARD LAWRENCE
1864-1939   D.S.O.   Josiah Clement   b. 1873
            1863-1916 Lord Wedgwood of Barlaston,   (Josiah Wedgwood & Sons, Inc.,
                       D.S.O., P.C., M.P.   of America)

DORIS AUDREY   JOSIAH   HENSLEIGH CECIL
b. 1894   Retired 1928 b. 1899   b. 1908
                        (Managing Director   (Josiah Wedgwood & Sons, Inc.,
                        from 1930)   of America)

CLEMENT TOM   JOHN HAMILTON
b. 1907   b. 1907

Note: Names in Capitals connected with the firm.

WEDGWOOD

EARLY DAYS

In examining the history of English pottery, attention is naturally drawn to the county of Staffordshire, which has, from very early times, been peculiarly associated with this craft. There are two essentials for making pottery: clay and fuel, and as long as firewood was plentiful, there was no particular reason why Staffordshire should have become the pottery center. But as the 17th century progressed, a growing scarcity of wood for such purposes and an increasing use of coal as fuel is found; it is therefore natural that pot-making began to flourish in this county, which was blessed with abundant supplies of both commodities.

It is quite probable that potting was carried on in this neighborhood even in Roman times, but the first historical evidence we have is in the Tunstall Court Rolls of 1350 in which are listed certain taxpayers with such names as William le Pottere, Robert le Potter and Thomas Throgher (thrower) which indicates that pottery was attaining significance as a local industry.

The type of ware made by these early potters was very rude indeed, and was made from local clay of marl which burned red or yellow and was probably purely utilitarian. In order to make it impervious to water, it was dusted with crude lead ore which melted in the firing process to form a glaze.

By 1650 there were many potteries in the district making butter pots, tygs or handled drinking vessels and other common types of ware, but at the same time we also find the first attempts at decorating. This was usually done by taking various colored slips or liquid clays and running them over the surface of the ware through a quill, somewhat like icing a cake. It was primitive, but had a charm of its own and represented a definite step forward in the evolution of the potter's art. The names most closely associated with this slip ware are Thomas and Ralph Toft, some of whose examples have survived, usually dated to commemorate some special occasion such as a wedding.

It is about this time that we begin to find Wedgwoods associated with the local craft, for, in a very early document of Gilbert Wedgwood dated 1649, he describes himself as a potter. We know little about Gilbert (1588-1678), but the fact that he came to Burslem, then the only town of any size in the Potteries, and lived at the Overhouse in 1612. His son Thomas later bought

Plate 1. Portrait of Josiah Wedgwood, by Sir Joshua Reynolds, 1783.

land in Burslem and built a small factory complete with workshops, sheds and a horsemill. This factory was set up next door to Burslem Church and was therefore known as the Churchyard Works. These early Wedgwoods, like their neighbors who were also engaged in the business, made a black ware known as Egyptian black by staining the clay with manganese dioxide or "magnus," and the somewhat better-known "variegated" wares such as marbled and tortoiseshell. The variegated wares were decorated by laying on lines and splashes of color and then combing or sponging them together, or, as in the case of agate ware by taking different colored clays and kneading them together; some beautiful effects were obtained and the wares show a great deal of originality and invention.

12

In 1685 first mention is made of Thomas Miles of Shelton who was making what was described as stoneware, which was later to become such an important feature of the Staffordshire potters. Stoneware was produced by mixing fine white sand with the local clays and firing the piece to such a high temperature that it became vitreous. It is due to a lawsuit in 1639 that we know that Gilbert Wedgwood's son Aaron and Aaron's sons Dr. Thomas and Richard were also engaged in the making of stoneware, but it was not until somewhat later, after the invention of salt glaze, that a peak of perfection was reached.

Another important figure of the period was John Dwight of Fulham (1637-1703) whose particular specialty was the making of red teapots as well as stoneware. He and the mysterious brothers John and David Elers, who turned up in the district from Amsterdam, 1693, contributed greatly to the improvement of the local product by the refinement of clays by sifting them

Plate 2, Nos. 310, 309, 312. *Left,* jug, rosso antico, unglazed, Etruria 1769. Height 3". *Center,* posset cup, made by Wedgwoods prior to Josiah, dark colored body, slip decoration, circa 1700. Height 4". *Right,* teapot, red ware, unglazed, sprigged decoration, early 18th century. Height 2¼".

to remove dirt and foreign matter, by the use of the turning lathe to obtain uniformity and precision in their shapes and, most important of all, by the introduction into England of the use of salt glaze.

Salt glazing was commonly practiced on the continent of Europe, particularly in Germany, and all evidence now points to the fact that it was the Elers brothers who brought the secret with them to England. The process consisted of firing the ware to a temperature much higher than that in common use for earthenware, and then, when red-hot, shovelling common salt into the top of the kiln; the salt fumes passed through holes in the saggar or fireclay box which protected the ware from the flames, and deposited a fine colorless soda glaze on the surface of the ware.

This was the precursor of the fluid lead glaze invented by Enoch Booth about 1750, which was made of flint, borax, lead, soda, etc., suspended in

Plate 3, Nos. 12, 11, 10. Pistol handled knives and fork, decorated handles with marbling, 1757-1766, excavated Whieldon site 1925.

Plate 4, Nos. 4, 18, 3. *Left,* teapot, open marbling, lead glaze, line of white slip applied to cover, Whieldon-Wedgwood 1755, excavated Whieldon site 1925. Height 3¼". *Center,* teapot, agate ware with fine marbling, unglazed, Whieldon-Wedgwood 1756, excavated Whieldon site 1925. Height 4". *Right,* teapot, open marbling with splashes of on-glaze color using metallic oxides, copper and manganese; Whieldon-Wedgwood 1755, excavated Whieldon site 1925. Height 4¾".

water. The ware was first of all given a "biscuit" or hardening fire and was then dipped in the fluid glaze and given a second or "glost" fire, which melted the glaze and covered the piece with a smooth and transparent film.

Salt glazed stoneware never reached perfection however until a man named Astbury appeared on the scene a few years after 1693. His great contribution was the introduction of white Devonshire clay into the "body" or clay mixture, and later, the addition of calcined and ground flint. The body made by Dwight and the Wedgwoods was dark or drab in color and did not show off the salt glaze to the best advantage, but with the whitening of the body the foundation was laid for the preëminence of this most important product of the Potteries, and also, at a later date, for Josiah Wedgwood's cream color ware which was eventually to supersede it.

Thus a gradual evolution took place, and definite advances were made over the early slip and variegated wares, even though these remained the staple products of the district. Hereafter new inventions came rapidly. The

Plate 5, No. 31. Cream jug, open marbling, unglazed, Whieldon-Wedgwood 1756. Height 2½".

use of plaster of Paris molds, for instance, opened the way for far more complicated shapes than could be made by hand or on the lathe and entailed the services of such specialists as moldmakers, casters, pressers, and stoukers who attach spouts and handles. Ancillary trades began to spring up, such as the "spur" and "thimble" makers, who made small bits of fired clay which were used to separate pieces of ware in the glost fire to prevent their sticking together.

The trade was becoming too complicated to be handled by a Jack-of-all-trades and we see the beginning of specialization and the transition of the master potter to a capitalist. The raw materials were at hand and the necessary skilled labor was becoming available in the area. It was at this point that Josiah Wedgwood, who more than any one man changed the history of the potteries, appeared on the scene. He was able to build on the foundations laid by such men as Elers and Astbury, as well as upon four generations of his own family who had been potting in Burslem from about 1612.

JOSIAH WEDGWOOD

Josiah Wedgwood was born in 1730 and was the youngest and thirteenth child of Thomas and Mary Wedgwood of the Churchyard House. His father, who does not seem to have been particularly successful, died when Josiah was only nine years old, leaving a legacy of £20 to each of his seven surviving children.

The young lad was sent to school between the ages of six and nine in Newcastle-under-Lyme under the tutelage of a Mr. Blunt whose reports said that the young schoolboy "was a fair arithmetician and master of a capital hand." He was popular among his schoolmates and was possessed of a good deal of charm and humor.

He and his sisters set up a sort of museum in one of his father's work sheds which contained fossils, shells and other curiosities. This interest in shells lasted to his later life as we shall note from the influence which they exerted on some of his designs.

In 1744, after the death of his father he went to work for his elder brother, Thomas, at the Churchyard Works inherited from his father, and five years later Josiah became his brother's apprentice to learn the "art, mistery, occupation or imployment of throwing and turning," as recorded in Josiah's indenture to his brother Thomas.

Plate 6, Nos. 33, 49, 34. *Left,* teapot, biscuit, tortoiseshell glazed cover, crabstock handle and spout, applied ornamentation, Whieldon-Wedgwood 1758, excavated Whieldon pottery site, September 1924. Height 3½". *Right,* mold for making leaf design for applied decoration on teapot, excavated at Whieldon-Wedgwood site, 1924. *Center,* mold for spout excavated at Whieldon-Wedgwood site, 1924.

When he was eleven, Josiah suffered an attack of smallpox which effected his right knee and in later life his leg had to be amputated. But in some respects this disability had its compensations for he had to give up his work as a thrower and turn his attention to modeling and mold making. This gave him an opportunity for reading, research and experiment which afforded him a much broader training than he otherwise would have had.

At the end of his apprenticeship in 1749, Josiah suggested to his brother that he should become his partner in order to continue his experiments, but Thomas refused this proposal. He therefore went into partnership, in 1752, with John Harrison who had invested money in a pot-bank at Stoke which had previously belonged to Thomas Alders and here they turned out agate knife handles and buttons. Apparently the two men had disagreements and the arrangement was cancelled after a year's duration.

Plate 8, Nos. 50, 43. *Left,* teapot and cover, cauliflower pattern, Burslem 1760. Height 7". *Right,* model for teapot cover.

Plate 7, No. 49a. Plate, green glaze, vine and strawberry pattern, Whieldon-Wedgwood, 1759. Diameter 8¾".

18

Plate 9, Nos. 46, 45, 47, 48. *Left,* teapot and cover, cabbage pattern, green glaze, 1759. Height 5". *Left Center,* model for teapot spout in leaf pattern, salt glazed cream ware. *Right Center,* model for cream jug, cabbage pattern, salt glazed cream ware. *Right,* cream jug, cabbage pattern, green glaze, 1759. Height 2½".

In 1754 a new and more important partnership was started with Thomas Whieldon of Fenton Low. These two were congenial as Whieldon had the same curiosity and love of experiment as Josiah. He was a potter of considerable taste and had built up a good business in the marbled and agate types of ware which were at that time such a popular feature of the neighborhood.

During this partnership Josiah started what he termed his "experiment book" in which he recorded all the trials made in his effort to improve the glazes and bodies in use at that time. The preface, quoted below, illustrates quite clearly the state of trade, the types of ware made, and so on:

"This suite of Experiments was begun at Fenton Hall, in the parish of Stoke-on-Trent, about the beginning of the year 1759, in my partnership with Mr. Whieldon, for the improvement of our manufacture of earthenware, which at the time stood in great need of it, the demand for our goods decreasing daily, and the trade universally complained of as being bad and in a declining condition.

19

"White Stone Ware was the principal article of our manufacture. But this had been made a long time, and the prices were now reduced so low, that the potters could not afford to bestow much expense upon it or to make it so good in any respect as the ware would otherwise admit of. And with regard to Elegance of form, that was an object very little attended to.

"The next article in consequence to Stone Ware was an imitation of Tortoise-shell. But as no improvement had been made in this branch for several years, the country was grown weary of it; and though the price had been lowered from time to time in order to increase the sale, the expedient did not answer, and something new was wanted, to give a little spirit to the business.

"I had already made an imitation of Agate, which was esteemed beautiful and a considerable improvement, but people were surfeited with wares of these varie-gated colours.

"These considerations induced me to try for some more solid improvements, as well in the Body, as the Glazes, the Colours, and the Forms, of the articles of our manufacture.

"I saw the field was spacious, and the soil so good as to promise an ample recompense to any one who should labour diligently in its cultivation."

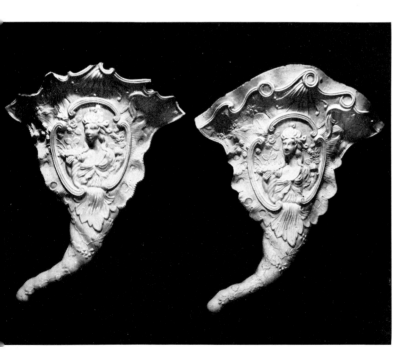

Plate 10, Nos. 39, 38. *Left,* cornucopia, salt glaze, Burslem 1760. Height 12". *Right,* model, salt glaze, used for cornucopia.

Plate 11, No. 60a. Vase, black basalt, encaustic painting, Etruria 1780. Height 11″.

Plate 12, No. 59a. Vase and cover, black basalt, encaustic decoration. Thrown and turned by Josiah Wedgwood and Thomas Bentley on the first day at Etruria, June 13, 1769. Height 10".

Experiment No. 7 in this book records the invention of green glaze which has remained popular to the present day. Not only was this glaze applied to plates and compotiers, but also to the famous pineapple and cauliflower tea sets, which can be considered Josiah's first success.

The partnership with Whieldon was terminated in 1759 because Wedgwood decided to go into business for himself. He rented from his uncles, Thomas and John, a small factory called the "Ivy House" consisting of two kilns, sheds, workrooms and a small cottage, for which he paid them an annual rental of £10. Josiah engaged his cousin Thomas, a journeyman, for five years at £22 per annum.

While he continued to make his cauliflower ware, Josiah began experiments in the perfection of cream color ware in 1760, which was ultimately to make his name famous. These experiments produced a cream-colored ware which was superior from every point of view to the earlier salt glaze made by his ancestors and other contemporary potters.

This early cream color "Useful" ware was decorated with simple designs, done at first by Widow Warburton at Hot Lane. In these designs Josiah's love of nature can be seen in the type of flower motifs which were produced.

Wedgwood's earlier shapes have that simplicity of design and perfection of detail which have enabled them to stand the test of time. His potting was so exact and his standards so high that this cream color ware has not been surpassed. He realized the importance of what is now termed functionalism: in other words, he insisted that lids should fit, that spouts should pour, and that handles should be comfortable to the hand.

In 1755 Sadler and Green of Liverpool invented the method of printing designs on glazed ware. These two men set up a business for decorating ware by means of transfers from copper plate engravings, and Wedgwood used to send his ware to Liverpool by pack horse to be thus decorated and then returned to Burslem. In the course of one of his frequent visits to Liverpool Josiah first met his life-long friend and eventual partner, Thomas Bentley.

The success of the cream color ware was immediate and widespread in spite of the fact that the area in which the potteries were situated was some-

Plate 13, No. 77. Teapot, black basalt, widow knob, Etruria 1778. Height 4″.

what off the map and communications extraordinarily difficult. In 1765, for instance, we hear of a friend who reported that, at a dinner with Lord Gower, Wedgwood's "potworks were the subject of conversation for some time, the Cream Color table services in particular. . . . His Lordship said that nothing of the sort could exceed them for fine glaze."

Josiah Wedgwood had achieved such acclaim that in the same year he received his first order from Royalty, a caudle service for Queen Charlotte, wife of George III. Josiah jokingly said that he obtained this commission "because nobody else would undertake it," but in fact it was probably due far more to his preëminence in the production of cream color tableware. As a result of the commission, he was allowed to style himself potter to the Queen and to christen this product Queen's Ware.

Wedgwood's business spread with rapidity throughout the British Isles and on the Continent of Europe, even to Russia. In 1763, in order to take care of his expanding business he moved to the Brick House or Bell Works, so termed because he adopted the unusual precedent of summoning his people to work by means of a bell rather than a horn.

Plate 14. Nos. 66, 65. *Left,* inkstand, black basalt, encaustic painting, Etruria 1778. Height 3½". *Right,* cup and saucer, black basalt, encaustic painting, Etruria 1778. Height 2¼".

Plate 15, No. 86. Vase, black basalt, applied fishtail handle, Etruria 1775. Height 10½″.

Plate 16, No. 76. Stirrup cup, hare's head, black basalt, Etruria 1782. Height 5½".

Plate 17, No. 71. Vase, black basalt, Etruria 1782. Height 9¼".

Two years later, he opened his first London showroom under the direction of his brother John which added to his growing reputation, and in 1774 a dinner and dessert service for the Empress Catherine of Russia was completed. This was in many ways Josiah's greatest undertaking in Queen's Ware for the set consisted of 952 pieces, each decorated with a different hand-painted view of the stately homes, castles and abbeys of England. It will be realized what a tremendous task this was considering the fact that photography had not been invented. There were 1244 views painted on this service, which necessitated the employment of a large corps of artists who covered the length and breadth of the British Isles making the necessary sketches. The total cost, including the artists' work and enamel painting, was £2410, but the profit was extremely small. However, Josiah realized the advertising value of this important commission and took full advantage of it by placing the entire service on exhibition at the new London showroom in Greek Street before it was sent to Russia. Queen Charlotte paid a visit of inspection, and the London rooms became the meeting place of the fashionable ladies of the time.

In 1766 Wedgwood proposed partnership with Thomas Bentley which was formally agreed to in 1769. Thus began a unique friendship which lasted until Bentley's death in 1780. Bentley was a man of wide culture and education who spoke French and Italian and had a vast knowledge of Classical and Renaissance art. It is fortunate indeed that the almost daily correspondence between these two men, which reflected every difficulty and success, has been preserved, since it throws an important light on the minutest details of the business during the course of the years 1769-1780. Besides giving a complete biographical sketch, these letters reveal an unusual charm of character in both men. As Wedgwood once remarked: "The very feel of your letters, even before the seal is broke, cheers my heart and does me good. They inspire me

Plate 18, No. 60. Teapot and cover, black basalt, encaustic painted decoration, Etruria 1778. Height 5½".

with a taste for emulation and everything that is necessary for the production of fine things." Bentley took charge of the Greek Street showrooms, getting orders, suggesting designs and also supervising the painting at the Chelsea studios, which had been set up to cope with the tremendous demand for decorated ware. It was through Bentley that Wedgwood made many important friends such as Priestly, the scientist, and Matthew Boulton, later a partner of James Watt, who supplied Wedgwood with an engine turning lathe in 1763.

An interesting sidelight on Josiah's continuous research for finer and more suitable raw materials is given by the Journal of a Mr. Griffiths who was sent to South Carolina in the year 1767 for white clay. Josiah Wedgwood had heard through one of his many contacts that the Cherokee Indian territory in South Carolina had produced a very fine white earth known as "ayoree" which was used by the Indians for making pipes. He was not satisfied until a personal investigation had been made and Mr. Griffiths was therefore commissioned to go in search of this clay and bring back samples. His diary is of immense interest, throwing light on conditions at that time and recounting the experiences which he encountered in bringing back five tons of clay.

Plate 19, Nos. 67, 79. *Left,* pen tray, black basalt, Wedgwood and Bentley, Etruria 1769. Rare script mark "Wedgwood & Bentley." Height 3". *Right,* lamp and cover, black basalt, engine turned and decorated, first indication of Wellesley embossment; Etruria 1782. Height 6½".

Plate 20, No. 92. Vase, black basalt, hand applied ornaments, Wedgwood and Bentley, Etruria 1775. Height 10¼".

Actually, it was found to be of fairly good quality, but the Cornish clays were superior in every respect and could be obtained more simply and cheaply. The South Carolina clay was therefore never imported to any extent, but this expedition indicates Josiah's determination to exhaust every possibility in order to make his product as perfect as possible.

The success of his wares had become so widespread and the demand so great that further expansion was necessary and in 1766 he therefore bought what was known as the Ridge House estate for £3,000 where he decided to build a new house and factory to be named "Etruria," in memory of the old Etruscan pottery in Italy.

ETRURIA PERIOD

The Etruria works were opened on July 13, 1769 and six black basalt vases were made to commemorate the event. With his partner, Bentley, turning the wheel, they were thrown by Josiah himself and were painted with red classical figures in imitation of the Etruscan models. They were inscribed "Artes Etruriae Renascuntur" (The Arts of Etruria are re-born).

The old Bell Works at Burslem were kept under the management of Thomas Wedgwood for the production of useful wares, and at first only the ornamental ware was made at Etruria. However, the Bell Works were closed four years later and the whole operation moved to the new factory. The principal production was, of course, the cream color ware which was made in a great variety of useful and ornamental pieces. At the same time many improvements were being made in other types which are generally classified as dry bodies because they are unglazed. The most important of these was the black basalt, a refinement of the Egyptian black which other Staffordshire potters had previously made in a somewhat cruder form.

Plate 21, No. 102. Plaque, black basalt, slightly bronzed, Etruria 1781. Diameter 15".

Plate 22, No. 109. Plaque for chimney piece, black basalt, *The Death of a Roman Warrior*, Etruria 1782. Height 11⅛", length 20⅛".

We have mentioned already that the black ware was made by staining the body with manganese dioxide, but with various improvements which Josiah made in this body, the black was richer in hue, finer in grain, and smoother in surface than any which had been made heretofore. In Wedgwood's catalogue of 1779, he describes basalt as "fine black porcelaine having nearly the same properties as the natural basalt, resisting the attacks of acids, being a touchstone to copper, silver and gold, and admitting of a good polish." When finally perfected, he wrote to Bentley to say that "the Black is sterling and will last for ever," a remarkably true prophecy considering its continuous popularity, down to the present day.

An enormous number of ornamental pieces were made in this body; vases, busts, medallion portraits, seals and intaglios. The more important vases were often decorated with red classical figures such as those made on the first day's throwing at Etruria, which were decorated in encaustic colors. These pieces were meant to imitate the newly excavated Etruscan vases, but the demand for them was limited and more and more there was a tendency toward the use of classical forms and ornamentation.

Perhaps Wedgwood's chief fame was the final perfection of what he termed his jasper body which is so well-known, that it hardly needs an explanation. This invention was the result of a long series of experiments to perfect a better medium for the reproduction of classical ornaments. The trial pieces that have been preserved run to over 10,000, and Josiah himself bitterly regretted that he had not kept his earlier examples.

The key to this success was eventually the discovery of a material known as cauk, or barium sulphate. When introduced into the paste, this gave a perfectly white hard stoneware which would take such a high fire that it became vitreous in a manner somewhat similar to porcelain. By the admixture of

Plate 23, No. 94a. Bust of Pindar, black basalt, Wedgwood and Bentley, Etruria 1777. Height 19½".

Plate 24, Nos. 97, 99. *Left,* medallion, black basalt, Mary Queen of Scots, Etruria 1772. Diameter 2". *Right,* medallion, black basalt, Jean Jacques Rousseau, Etruria 1768-1780. Diameter 1¾".

Plate 25, No. 211a. Vase and cover, sage green and white jasper, *Sacrifice to Hymen* and *Marriage of Cupid and Psyche,* Etruria 1776. Height 8¼".

Plate 26, No. 160. Vase, blue and white jasper, *Apotheosis of Homer,* modeled 1785 by John Flaxman, Etruria. Height 18".

coloring oxides to this paste it could be delicately stained in pale blue, sage green, yellow, dark blue, black and other colors. This formed the body of the piece and upon it were laid ornaments, usually in white, which were made in separate molds and "sprigged" on, or applied. Wedgwood himself, who knew of the labors that went into its invention, prized the jasper body above any of his other productions.

Quite apart from the fine vases and tablets produced, the jasper body was also used for a large series of historically important portrait medallions of

Plate 27, No. 210a. Vase, white jasper, applied decoration, plinth applied at a later date, *Maternal Affection,* modeled by William Hackwood, Etruria 1783. Height 12".

kings, queens, statesmen, scientists, inventors and "illustrious moderns," most of them modeled by Hackwood and Flaxman.

Wedgwood's great achievement was the reproduction of the Portland Vase, which is of such interest that a brief historical explanation will not be out of place. The original of this vase was excavated from a tomb outside Rome sometime between the years 1625 and 1644 together with a sarcophagus. The latter was placed in the museum in the Capitol in Rome. The vase itself, however, found its way into the library of the Barberini family where it continued to be one of the outstanding pieces of this collection for over one hundred years. It was eventually purchased in Rome by Sir William Hamilton, who in turn sold it at auction in 1786 to the Duchess of Portland. Knowing of Josiah's interest in reproducing antiquities, the Duke placed the vase at his disposal and after four years of experiment to get the color, surface and texture correct he was able to state that he had succeeded. In 1790 the

34

copy was presented for approval and was declared by Sir Joshua Reynolds, President of the Royal Academy, "to be a correct and faithful imitation both in the general effect and the most minutest details of the parts."

The number of copies of the Portland Vase made by Wedgwood is uncertain but there is evidence that there were twenty-six subscribers to the first edition who paid prices varying between twenty and thirty guineas. A model maker named Webber was responsible for the reliefs. The original vase is now in the Gem Room of the British Museum; it was unfortunately smashed to pieces in 1848 by a madman but was subsequently pieced together with the greatest care.

So much success was attained by jasper ware that Wedgwood was troubled continually by rival potters who pirated his ideas and designs. The famous blue ground with white figures is so universally known and recognized as Wedgwood that it should be pointed out that there were many other copyists of his work at that time and ever since. For example two of his contempo-

Plate 28, No. 212a. Teapot, blue and white jasper, *Infant Academy*, designed by Sir Joshua Reynolds, Etruria 1778. Height 6".

raries, Neale and Palmer, were such a nuisance that he cautioned Bentley not to allow anyone else to see designs which were sent to him for inspection and approval. From some correspondence which passed between these two men, it is seen that they finally came to the conclusion there was nothing they could do and that it was perhaps preferable to "be released from these degrading, slavish chains; these mean, selfish fears of other people copying my work. Rather we should throw out all the hints we can and have half the artists of Europe working after our models. This would be noble and would suit both our dispositions and sentiments much better than narrow, mercenary, selfish channels."

While the cream color, basalt and jasper wares formed the staple lines of Etruria's output, some of the other important dry bodies which were pro-

Plate 29, No. 221. Teapot and cover, green and white jasper, Acanthus and Bell applied decoration, Etruria 1789. Height 6½".

Plate 30, No. 173. Inkstand, blue and white jasper, column made to imitate a Roman ruin, Etruria 1786. Height 4".

duced in great quantity such as the rosso antico—a refinement of the "red porcelaine" of Elers, the cane ware (buff in color), the drab, chocolate and olive wares must not be overlooked. All of these were made basically from local marls with additions of coloring oxides or "ocherous earths" to give them the right hue.

Plate 31, No. 224. Teapot and cover, drab jasper, applied decoration in chocolate, Sacrifice Figure, Etruria 1789. Height 5⅛".

A variety of shapes, both useful and ornamental, were made in these bodies such as teapots, jugs, bough pots for plants and flowers, inkstands, lamps, busts, portrait medallions, comporters and so on. The cane was made in imitation of bamboo and piecrust, the latter being used extensively in the 1800's in order to save flour in times of scarcity. In the "Life of George [Beau] Brummell" by Captain Jeffs (1844) is found, "The scarcity two years after Brummell's retirement, viz. in 1800, was so great that the consumption of flour for pastry was prohibited in the Royal Household, rice being used instead. The distillers left off malting; hackney coach fares were raised 25%, and Wedgwood made dishes to represent pie crust."

Plate 32, Nos. 223, 220. *Left,* biscuit model of teapot on right. *Right,* teapot and cover, green and white jasper, Sacrifice Figure, Etruria 1790. Height 5½".

Whereas many of these shapes were plain, others were decorated with colored designs sprigged on, giving a contrast between body and ornament, especially in the case of the drab body which was embellished with chocolate or blue reliefs.

It is not generally known that Josiah Wedgwood also brought out a "composition" body, a very hard and vitreous type of stoneware, for the making of mortars and pestles. These have been made continuously to the present day and are referred to by M. Veldhuysen, Wedgwood's Amsterdam agent, in the following terms (1780):

"That your mortars resist the strongest acids was incredible history to several physicians, and therefore they have carefully examined them with the strongest spirit of sea salt (Spiritus Salis Marini), the consequences of it was that your mortars endured said acid and any others and therefore the physicians thought it necessary to make it known in their annals (which I assure you they have very elegantly done) but likewise that I should make mention of it in the explanation of the mortars, which you will perceive, I have not omitted. From these circumstances I am convinced that the sale will be considerable with me, and therefore I beg you to forward very soon the order of them."

The large list of bodies produced as the result of Wedgwood's inventive mind, would not be complete without mention of pearl ware. Pearl came as the result of complaints from some customers about the varying shades of cream color ware — a condition which was likely to occur, particularly in those days, as the result of variations in raw materials and firing techniques. Several shades of cream were intentionally made by the judicious admixture of iron oxide to the glaze, the hues varying from a pale cream to straw or saffron; but these variations were in the glaze and not in the body. Eventually

Plate 33, No. 219. Cup and saucer, can shape, green and white jasper, Etruria 1790. Height of cup $2\frac{9}{16}''$, diameter of saucer $4\frac{1}{2}''$.

the demand for a white body became so great that pearl was introduced — not that it was ever manufactured on the vast scale of cream but it was important as being the precursor of the durable white granite wares made later by such potters as Maddock, Meakin, and Grindley. Pearl contained a greater proportion of flint and white clay than cream color, and a small percentage of cobalt oxide was added to the glaze to give the same effect as "blueing" does in laundry. Some delightful figurines were made in pearl body which, though not very well known, nevertheless have much artistic merit.

Plate 34, Nos. 214, 215, 211. *Left,* teapot and cover, blue and white jasper, *Domestic Employment,* designed by Lady Templetown, Etruria 1788. Height 5½". *Center,* tray, blue and white jasper, Etruria 1788. Diameter 13¾". *Right,* cup and saucer, blue and white jasper, Maternal Subject, designed by Lady Templetown, Etruria, 1784. Height of cup 2". Diameter of saucer 5⅛".

Plate 35, No. 196a. Bulb pot, sage green and white jasper, Etruria 1778. Height 7½".

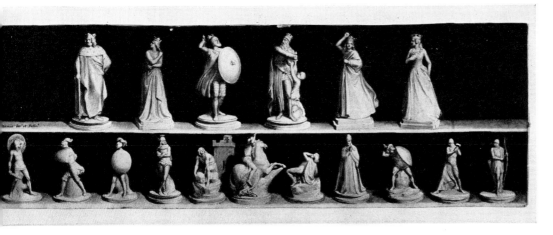

Plate 36, No. 111. Drawing for chessmen by John Flaxman. 1784.

At left: Plate 37, No. 116. Wedgwood chessmen, modeled by Arnold Machin, 20th century, *from left to right*: Rosso antico king, Black basalt king, Colored body lavender Queen's Ware king, Queen's Ware king.

Plates 38 and 39, No. 119. 18th century Wedgwood chessmen. *From left to right*: Wax model of king, Clay model of king, Finished white jasper king, White jasper king on blue jasper dip base.

Plate 40, No. 144. Medallion, blue and white jasper, *Sir Joshua Reynolds,* modeled by John Flaxman, Etruria 1780. Diameter 4½".

Plate 41, No. 168. Plaque, blue and white jasper, *Choice of Hercules,* modeled 1777 by William Hackwood, Etruria. Diameter 9½".

Plate 42, Nos. 128, 126, 125. *Left,* medallion, blue and white jasper, *Diomedes,* Etruria 1777. Diameter 3". *Center,* wax model and *Right,* biscuit model.

WEDGWOOD-THE SCIENTIST

Quite apart from Wedgwood's achievements as a potter his public life merits attention, for he rose from humble beginnings and by his own enterprise became one of the most interesting figures of his age, the friend of artists, scientists and politicians, the leader in his industry and the founder of a tradition which has survived for two centuries.

Mention has been made of his limited education, the difficulties of his early years, his poor health and his lack of capital. Yet, as William Burton has said, "His influence was powerful, and his personality so dominant, that all other English potters worked on the principles he had laid down, and thus a fresh impulse and a new direction was given to the potters of England and of

Plate 43, Nos. 132, 141, 149. Medallions, blue and white jasper, Etruria 1780. *Left,* head of Emperor Augustus. Height 3¾". *Center, Sportive Love,* designed by Lady Templetown. Height 4⅝". *Right,* Benjamin Franklin. Height 4".

the civilized world. He is the only potter of whom it may truly be said that the whole subsequent course of pottery manufacture has been influenced by his individuality, skill and taste."

This influence may be attributed largely to the painstaking thoroughness of his research, his constant desire for improvement and his insistence upon perfection. The sciences of chemistry and physics were in their infancy during

43

Plate 44, No. 162. Plaque, blue and white jasper, *Dancing Hours*, one of two companion plaques, modeled by John Flaxman, 1775. Originally in the nude, they were draped by William Hackwood. Etruria 1777. Height 5⅝″, Length 18⅜″.

his lifetime — in fact it was only in 1774, five years after his death, that his friend Priestly discovered oxygen — and yet one glance at his experiment book will show why he was successful in discovering the principles of ceramic manufacture that are taken for granted today. It necessitated over 10,000 trials to perfect the jasper body — a result which today could easily have been achieved by the application of the principles of modern science.

A good example of his originality is his invention of the pyrometer for measuring high temperatures, which ultimately won for him the coveted Fellowship of the Royal Society. It was of the greatest importance to be able to gauge the heat of ovens for firing in order to obtain the best results — and yet no known thermometer would register the tremendous temperatures used in firing.

Plate 45, No. 145, 143. Medallions, blue and white jasper, Queen Charlotte and George III of England, Etruria 1780. Height 3¼″.

It was common knowledge that clay contracted upon being heated, but the significance of this fact escaped most people—namely, that there was a definite relationship between temperature and contraction. By taking small cylindrical bits of clay of standard composition and diameter, it was easy to measure how much they had contracted at various temperatures by sliding them down a V-shaped scale. The principle of this pyrometer is still often used today in its modern application—contraction rings.

Josiah's knowledge of science was well in advance of that possessed by his competitors, and was due partly to his stated belief that "everything yields to experiment," and partly to his friendships with such men as Dr. Erasmus Darwin, Priestley, Boulton and Watt, the leading scientists of the day. That he had no fear of trying out new inventions is shown by the fact that he corresponded with Matthew Boulton of Soho in 1768 concerning the introduction of the engine lathe by which geometric designs and flutings could be incised on his ware. This finally led to the building of an improved machine based upon these types used in Soho.

Also at this time his life-long friend Dr. Darwin was making plans and models for a windmill to grind colors. The plans were approved, but Darwin

Plate 46, No. 175 E. Plaque, blue and white jasper, *Birth of Bacchus*, modeled 1782 by John Flaxman, Etruria. Height 6".

Plate 47, No. 181. Custard cup, lilac and white jasper, shaped in mold, lattice work made separately in a pitcher mold and laid on cup, Etruria 1786. Height 1½".

counselled Wedgwood "to wait the Wheel-Fire-Engine, which goes on slowly," and, later, to wait until "he could learn in what forwardness Mr. Watt's Fire-Engine was in." These references were, of course, to James Watt's research into the application of steam to motive power. Apparently Wedgwood put his faith in Watt's machines and placed successive orders for their installation at Etruria. An important document has turned up within the last ten years showing that Wedgwood actually advanced £5,000 to Boulton to help him in his financial difficulties during the experimental stages of manufacturing Watt's engines at Soho.

Some steam pumps were in operation in the Cornish tin mines where they had replaced Newcomen's "atmospheric" engines, but it can now be shown that Etruria was the first factory to install a Watt engine, as early as 1782. This was replaced by others, and eventually Josiah II purchased a 30 h.p. model which was in use until 1912 and was, at that late date, a curiosity since it was worked with the "Sun and Planet" motion instead of a crank, and was said to be the only one of its kind in existence.

Plate 48, Nos. 177, 176. *Left*, canoe basket, three-color jasper, blue, white and yellow strap work, Etruria 1782. Height 5½". *Right*, biscuit model for basket.

Plate 49, Nos. 166, 184a, 166a. *Lower left,* hair brush (1880), with jasper cameo, designed by Lady Templetown, Etruria 1779. Height 2". *Upper Left,* patch box, ivory case mounted with cameo, *Cupids at Play,* Etruria 1778. Length 4". *Right,* perfume bottle, blue and white jasper, *Venus and Cupid,* Etruria 1778. Length 4½".

Plate 50, No. 184. Mascara box, ivory inlaid with blue, white and lavender jasper cameo of Antinous, Etruria 1788. Length 2⅞".

Plate 51, Nos. 191, 192. *Above,* earrings, blue and white jasper cameos, *Phaeton* and *Artemis,* cut steel setting, Etruria 1790. Height 3". *Below,* bracelet, blue and white jasper cameos, cut steel setting, Etruria 1790. Length 6½".

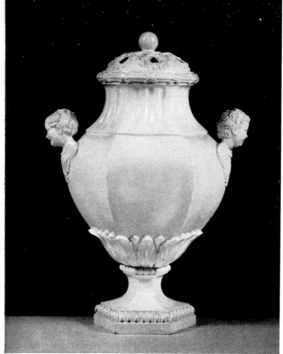

Plate 52, Nos. 53, 52. *Left*, vase with cover, early cream ware with lead glaze; Burslem 1765. Height 11″. *Right*, pear wood model for vase, carved by John Coward, Burslem 1765. Height 11″.

Plate 53, No. 178. Jug, blue and white jasper, diced design with green applied decoration, Etruria 1784. Height 4½″.

Plate 54, No. 341. Portland Vase, black and white jasper. This copy was number 25, made in 1793, the first vase was completed at Etruria in 1790.

WEDGWOOD — THE ARTIST

Whatever his other attributes, Wedgwood could not properly be described as an artist in the true sense of the word. He was born with innate taste and an appreciation of line and form which was always to stand him in good stead. But it was largely through the employment of the talents of others that his artistic fame was assured. He knew his limitations, and had the sound judgment to gather about him the very best artists of his day who were commissioned to translate his ideas into concrete form.

At the start of his career it was more than probable that he had a great deal to do with the designs, for before the industrialization of the potteries, it was the usual practice for the "Master" to be, not only his own designer, but his own modeler, clay-maker, thrower, stouker and fireman. Thus many

Plate 55, No. 229. Queen's Ware border designs from the original 1770 pattern book of Josiah Wedgwood and still used today.

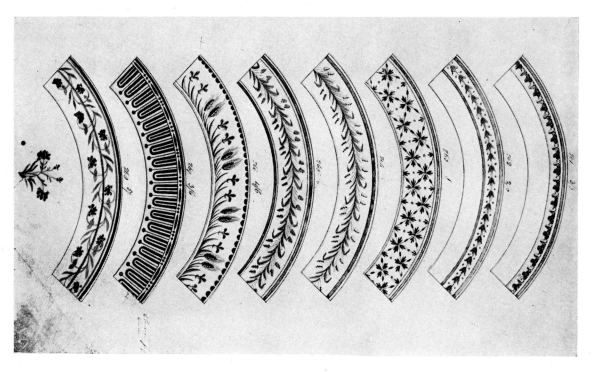

Plate 56, No. 272. Center for jelly mold, Queen's Ware, with flower decoration, Etruria 1774. Height 9″.

of the earlier shapes may be ascribed to Josiah himself, shapes such as the famous coffee set and tea set numbered 129 and 146 respectively in the first shape book. For purity of design and simplicity of form, these have never been surpassed and even today they satisfy the criteria of functional modern design. The early shape books are replete with drawings of equally distinguished pieces, as good by modern standards as they were in his day.

The same may be said of patterns. Many of the earlier dinnerware decorations were executed by Widow Warburton, prior to the setting up of the Chelsea Studios in London where the firm's own decorators were eventually trained in the Wedgwood tradition. But here again, the influence which Wedgwood exerted on the widow is noted, for in the 1759 pattern books is found a profusion of simple handpainted borders, using barley, the grape, the strawberry and so on, obviously inspired by his love of nature. His early collection of seaweeds, shells and fossils is also reflected in the Nautilus forms —a series of shell-shaped center pieces, flower holders and wall-brackets—

51

the Seaweed design and the imitations of agate, basalt and jasper stone.

   With the perfection of the basalt and jasper bodies the time had come when specialization was imperative, and obviously Josiah realized that the services of outside artists were necessary. Recognizing the importance of capitalizing on the current interest in neo-classical design, he engaged the services of one of the greatest contemporary artists, John Flaxman. Flaxman, a truly remarkable artist, had won the first prize of the Society of Arts when only twelve years of age, and at fifteen had exhibited at the Royal Academy which had recently been founded (1768). Apparently his first commission for Wedgwood was in 1775, after which he continued to turn out a prodigious number of drawings and models. Among Flaxman's masterpieces are the famous "Dancing Hours," "The Nine Muses," "Sacrifice to Cupid" and "Psyche Bound and Attacked by Cupid."

Plate 57, Nos. 233, 230. Designs for nut basket, *left,* and orange bowl, *right,* from Josiah's 1770 catalogue. See Plate 58 for finished examples.

Henry Webber, to whom are attributed the superb Portland Vase figures, was engaged in 1782 on the recommendation of Sir Joshua Reynolds, and in order to keep pace with the rapidly increasing demand for the classical, he and Flaxman were sent to Rome in 1787. There they founded a school of modelers who worked on the spot, adapting and copying designs and architectural details and submitting their work to Wedgwood for approval, as well as doing original work in the same tradition. Among these artists, were men such as Angelini, Dalmozzoni, Devere, and the famous gem cutter Pacetti who was responsible for the splendid "Sacrifice to Iphigenia," an adaptation of the reliefs on the Sarcophagus in which the Portland Vase was originally found.

The chief resident artists at Etruria were William Hackwood, who had been employed since the opening of the works, and William Wood. Hackwood was chiefly known for his work on ornamental wares, particularly jasper, while Wood concentrated on the useful wares. Of the two, Hackwood became better known because of his exquisite medallions and the more elaborate but equally beautiful "Seasons," "Judgment of Hercules" and the modeling of "Maternal Affection" designed by Lady Templetown. But apart from these masterpieces, Hackwood, and Wood as well, spent the bulk of their time at Etruria making the models from designs submitted by the Rome school and others, repairing, altering and carrying out the routine requirements of the factory.

Plate 58, Nos. 233, 230. *Left,* pierced nut basket, Queen's Ware, Etruria 1780. Height 3". *Right,* covered orange bowl, Queen's Ware, Etruria 1769. Height 9". See Plate 57.

In addition to the research carried out by these men, Josiah was constantly seeking new design material—borrowing books and prints, visiting private collections, spurring Bentley on to make use of his knowledge of classical and Renaissance art by searching treatises on these subjects, obtaining ideas from whatever sources were available. He worked with Matthew Boulton in Soho in the production of ornamental pieces mounted in metal—a natural partnership since both men were imbued with the idea of combining art and industry.

In short this desire for the improvement of industrial art was the guiding principle behind Wedgwood's search for the best work that could be obtained. Indeed many of his bodies were invented for the purpose of translating into his media the finest designs, whether original or copied from the great masters. His principles were sound, for not only were his ornamental pieces well adapted to their surroundings—the furniture of Sheraton and Hepplewhite and the architectural ornament of the Adam brothers—but his tableware shapes and designs set the standard of the day and, furthermore, started the "Living Tradition" of good design and good potting which has been followed ever since by the firm.

Plate 59, Nos. 235. Soup tureen, Queen's Ware, transfer printed Bewick Scenes, Burslem 1769. Height 10¾".

Plate 60, No. 307. Coffee pot, Queen's Ware, Shell Edge; Sadler and Green transfer print of Liverpool Birds in red, Etruria 1772. Height 8½″.

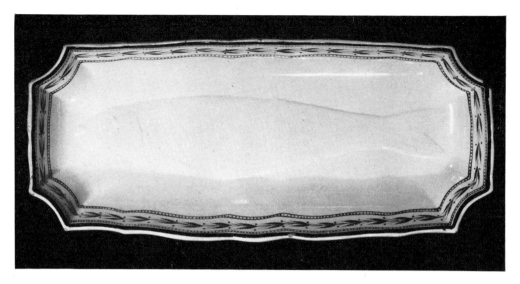

Plate 61, No. 251. Herring dish, Queen's Ware, purple border, Etruria 1769. Length 11¼".

The period in which Wedgwood lived and worked was, indeed, the golden age of English design. The work of the contemporary Georgian silversmiths and furniture makers needs no comment, except to point out that such men rightly earned their reputations as individual craftsmen, and their names have been handed down to posterity as individuals rather than as representatives of a period.

The interrelation between craftsmen in various trades was important, for while Wedgwood was taking advantage of the demand for classical decoration, he was working with his fellow craftsmen in other fields and co-ordinating his efforts with theirs.

Plate 62, No. 254. Bowl, Queen's Ware, yellow and brown decoration, Etruria 1775. Height 3½".

Above: Plate 63, Nos. 281, 462, 278. Queen's Ware shapes taken from Josiah Wedgwood's first pattern book of 1770: *Left,* Royal shape, no. 4 in pattern book, purple border, Etruria 1778, Diameter 10"; *Center,* Queen's shape, painted in purple husk design, Etruria 1770, Diameter 10"; *Right,* concave shape, no. 8 in pattern book, painted in red and black, Etruria 1790, Diameter 10".

Above right: Plate 64, No. 238. Dinner plate, Queen's Ware, sepia painted view of a ruin with green frog on the border, Etruria 1774. Diameter 10". Part of service made for Catherine the Great, Empress of Russia. The green frog was the symbol of the Russian Palace, "La Grenouillière" at Tsarskoje-Selo.

Plate 65, No. 288. Sandwich set, Queen's Ware, yellow, brown and red border, Etruria 1776. Height 5".

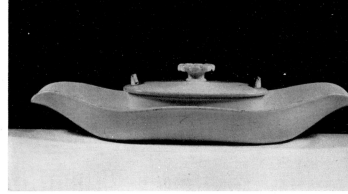

Plate 66, No. 480. Butter dish
and cover, fixed stand, Queen's
Ware, Etruria 1783. Height 3".

Plate 67, Nos. 276, 280, 282.
Queen's Ware shapes taken from
Josiah Wedgwood's first pattern
book of 1770: *Left*, shell edge
shape, no. 9, painted in blue
"Mared" pattern, Etruria 1770,
Diameter 10"; *Center*, feather
edge shape, no. 2, trial painting
in green, Etruria 1772, Diameter 10"; *Right*, feather edge
shape, no. 1, Sadler and Green
transfer print of Liverpool
Birds, Etruria 1770, Diameter 8".

Plate 68, Nos. 285, 325. *Left*, glacier,
Queen's Ware, pierced and relief
decoration, Etruria 1773. Height
10". *Right*, custard cup and cover,
Queen's Ware, painted green oak
leaf border with brown lines, Etruria 1775. Height 3¼".

WEDGWOOD – THE PROGRESSIVE

It is sometimes difficult to understand how Josiah Wedgwood was able to indulge his many outside interests while, at the same time, he was manager and mainspring of the Etruria enterprise. However this may be, he was the prime mover and leader in numerous projects to better conditions, not only for his own workpeople, but for the whole industry.

He soon realized that transport facilities must be improved if the pottery industry were to progress. The state of the roads was quite intolerable, being merely muddy cart tracks which were impassible even to wagons during the winter season. Raw materials were brought in, and finished goods taken out of the district on the backs of horses and donkeys, causing delay and breakage, while transport by river was hardly better.

Plate 69, No. 257. Bowl, Queen's Ware, lag and feather painted border, Etruria 1775. Height 4⅞".

Plate 70, No. 353. Sphinx letter weight, rosso antico on black basalt base, Etruria 1783. Height 4¼".

Plate 71, No. 359. Bough pot, rosso antico, engine turned, applied black ornaments, Etruria 1783. Height 7½".

There were turnpikes, for the use of which tolls were levied, but the nearest point at which the turnpike passed was at Newcastle-under-Lyme. In 1762 Wedgwood led his fellow potters to agitate for better conditions and to present a petition to Parliament. The results were satisfactory, for in 1763 a Bill for the construction of a road from Burslem to Liverpool was passed over the opposition of the Newcastle innkeepers who objected to such a by-passing of their establishments.

But even road transport was twice as expensive as that by water, and Wedgwood realized the necessity of a connection by the latter means with the main ports of North England for the import of materials and the export of finished goods to the Continent and the Americas. At this time the famous James Brindley, known as "The Schemer," was engineering the Bridgewater Canal, the first of its kind, and since he was well known in the potteries—having built a windmill to grind flints for Josiah's uncle, John Wedgwood — it is natural that Josiah proposed to him the possibility of joining the Trent and Mersey rivers, thus affording an outlet to the sea. In 1764 he was working for this project and getting Bentley to issue pamphlets in its support. A meeting was held in December, 1765, at which Brindley proved the feasibility of the plan, and it was decided to petition Parliament for the necessary powers. Wedgwood subscribed £1,000 and was elected Treasurer of the committee set up for the purpose of pursuing the project. An act of Parliament was obtained in 1766 and on July 26 Wedgwood cut the first sod before the citizens, who are said to have roasted a whole ox to celebrate the occasion. The 93 mile long canal, later known as the Grand Trunk, was completed in 1777 and proved to be an unqualified success, reducing freight rates to almost one-tenth of their former amount.

Plate 72, No. 357. Cream jug, rosso antico, applied decoration in black basalt, interior glaze, Etruria 1798. Height 2¾″.

These two examples of Wedgwood's foresight were based on sound business reasoning, but his liberality of ideas as well as his generosity, are amply illustrated by his support of and his financial assistance to the causes in which

Plate 73. Nos. 347, 362. *Left, vase, cane with drab ornaments, Etruria 1795. Height 6". Right,* mug, cane, *Cupid Returning from the Chase,* Etruria 1795. Height 4".

he believed. As an example, Wedgwood's name is found among the petition-
ers of Burslem in 1760 for "a small piece of land lying in Burslem, where
the Maypole did formerly stand, in order to erect a piece of building for a
Schoole, as there is but one Schoole in the Town, and for want of another,
two parts of the children out of three are put to work without any learning,
by reason the other Schoole is not sufficient to instruct them." Later, in 1792,
he subscribed handsomely to help the Polish people against Russian invasion.

He was a keen supporter of the American Revolution and wrote to Bentley, March 19, 1778, following the Declaration of Independence, that he
"bless'd his Stars and Lord North that America is free" as one refuge "from
the iron hand of Tyranny." He and Bentley were also keen supporters of the
Slave Emancipation Society and commissioned Hackwood in 1768 to model
the "Slave in Chains" cameo which was adopted as the seal of the Society.
A free thinker, Wedgwood, in a letter to Erasmus Darwin, 1789, "rejoiced in
the Glorious revolution which has taken place in France," even though it was
injurious to his business, and emphatically declared that "Every member of
the State must either have a vote or be a slave."

Although he did not know it, Josiah was one of the leaders of the Indus-

62

Plate 74, No. 375. Candlestick, variegated ware, marbling, Etruria 1770. Height 5¼″.

Plate 75, No. 379. Vase, variegated ware, sprinkled porphyry, black basalt plinth, Wedgwood and Bentley, Etruria 1772. Height 16".

trial Revolution which dawned with the invention of the steam engine. He lived in a time when industrialization was rapidly gaining pace around him — the master potter had evolved from a peasant craftsman to a capitalist employing, in some cases, hundreds of specialists; the pot bank had grown into a factory and the crafts from a little-known local business to a world-wide industry. But although the industrial revolution brought many abuses with the growth of the factory—poor working conditions, long hours and child labor—there still remained something of the paternalistic relationship between the "master" and his workers, particularly at Etruria. This was his model factory, Etruria Hall his elegant home, set in spacious surroundings, Etruria village the domicile of his workpeople. Thus began the "Living Tradition" of progress which was so scrupulously followed by his descendants when Josiah's works finally became outdated.

POST ETRURIA PERIOD

Josiah I died in 1795 after a painful illness, and his second son, Josiah II, inherited the Etruria estate and the works, with a quarter interest being held by Thomas Byerley, nephew of Josiah I. Byerley had taken quite an active part in the administration of the firm for some time prior to his uncle's death. He assumed full control of the management after Josiah II had more or less retired in the south of England, and visited Etruria only infrequently. The wars of the French Revolution and the Napoleonic Wars were disastrous to Continental trade, and business generally became so slack that in 1811 Josiah II wrote that "the business is not worth carrying on, and if I could withdraw my capital from it, I would tomorrow." Fortunately he did not do so, and in spite of the poor times, he and Byerley made considerable improvements to the Etruria works and embarked on the manufacture of bone china in 1812 to try to stimulate trade. Translucent china had been made by other Stafford-shire potters prior to this time — notably by the managers of the New Hall company — but although Josiah I had evidently carried out experiments in

Plate 76, Nos. 382, 372. *Left,* vase, variegated ware, agate, Wedgwood and Bentley, Etruria 1776. Height 8½". *Right,* bough pot, variegated ware, green sprinkled granite, applied decoration, Etruria 1783. Height 11".

65

this field, he had been discouraged from commercial production because of his difficulties with Richard Champion over patent rights to the use of china clay from Cornwall, which Champion had purchased from William Cookworthy in 1773.

Plate 77, Nos. 437, 438. *Left,* candlestick, cane with green and lilac applied ornamentation, smear glaze, Etruria 1830. Height 1¾". *Right,* vase, cane with blue applied ornamentation, Etruria 1820. Height 4¼".

After 1816, however, trade began to revive, and the manufacture of bone china was therefore discontinued until 1878. More attention was given in these years to the staple lines, of which Queen's ware and jasper appear to have been the most important. Designs and decorations maintained their previous high level, the original molds of Flaxman, Webber and the other great Wedgwood artists being used. As far as tableware was concerned, the Oriental influence began to appear during the first half of the 19th century and is very strongly marked in such patterns as Eastern Flowers, Palm, Groups, Willow, Horticultural and Nankin. Napoleon was supplied with an Ivy design during his exile on St. Helena, and a tremendous revival of

Color Plate II, No. 217. Bowl, lilac and white Jasper, *Domestic Employment* and *Boys at Play*, designed by Lady Templetown, Etruria 1784. Height 3″, Diameter 6⅜″.

Plate 77a, No. 391. Sugar bowl and cover, Queen's Ware, photographic print, Etruria 1878. Height 4½".

printed patterns occurred. Although Wedgwood never made the vast quantities turned out by their competitors, nevertheless their trade with America was considerable in the historical type of blue printed Staffordshire ware.

Early in the post-Etruria period lustre gained a good deal of popularity, not only as produced by the Wedgwood firm, but also as made by many other English potters. The discovery of platinum at the end of the 18th century opened the way for the use of this metal in pottery; finely divided and suspended in an oily base, it was applied either direct to the ware by the normal method of painting or as a resist. In the latter case a design was printed or painted in a resist material—usually china clay mixed with syrup or some such sticky medium—and the lustre applied over the surface of the piece. On firing the resist burned away, leaving the design in white and the rest of the piece solidly covered with silver. "Moonshine" lustre was another favorite and was prepared from gold salts, which, when fired, gave a copper sheen to the article to which it had been applied.

About 1828 trade seems again to have been depressed, the Wedgwood London showrooms were given up, and the stock of ware and molds held there was disposed of.

Josiah III joined the firm in 1823, but retired in 1842 just prior to the death of his father, Josiah II. Thenceforth Josiah II's third son, Francis, carried on the management. This period, 1840-1880, was one of rapid mechanization and many ideas were introduced for labor-saving—such scientific

Plate 78, No. 465. Wall pocket, Nautilus shape, overglaze moonshine lustre in purple, Etruria 1810. Height 6″.

advances as the filter press for drying clay, blungers for mixing and pugmills for preparing it. In this period, too, we find the beginnings of unionization on the part of the workers, who were gradually struggling to improve hours and working conditions.

Since 1777 great use had been made of jasper dip, or bas-relief ware. This was white stoneware which was dipped in jasper slip (liquid clay) so that only the surface was colored. White ornaments were then applied in the usual manner. Jasper dip remained in regular production for many years, but solid jasper was reintroduced in 1854 during one of the cycles of better trade. Other new bodies developed at this time were Parian and colored bodies. Parian was a hard paste porcelain made by the casting method and usually unglazed. It was so named because it resembled the marble of Paros. Even though Parian was made by Wedgwood for only a brief period, some remark-

Plate 79, No. 451. Teapot, stonewear smear glaze, Patrician design, Etruria 1830. Height 3".

ably fine busts and figures were produced in this medium, as well as some rather less successful groups of statuary. Colored bodies are of much greater importance since they have remained in popular favor to the present time and command an ever increasing interest because of their simplicity. These

70

Plate 80, No. 458. Biscuit model, hunt jug, still produced by Wedgwood, Etruria 1800. Height 5".

later bodies are composed of the regular cream-colored Queen's Ware stained with oxides to produce a delicate shade of sky blue known as"lavender," a sage-green called "celadon" and a buff "cane," somewhat similar in shade to the old dry-bodied cane, but glazed. All three colored bodies have been decorated with a large variety of patterns, but their chief charm is in the undecorated state in which their simplicity accentuates Josiah's "traditional" shapes, such as his teapot (146) and his coffee pot (129).

As a whole, the period was not one of great artistic merit — rather the reverse — colored bodies were a welcome contrast to the over-decorated and gaudily tinted monstrosities of the Victorian period. Rather typical of these creations were the majolica glazes introduced by Wedgwood in 1860. Majolica was a type of soft lead glaze which could be highly colored and which was used to decorate ornamental pieces, dessert ware and decorative slabs as well as dinnerware. Somewhat more restrained patterns in this glaze were carried out by Emile Lessore who had, at one time, worked at the Royal factory at Sèvres, and who joined Wedgwood in 1859.

Plate 81, No. 365. Game pie dish, cane, simulating pie crust, molded decoration, Etruria 1815. Height 4½".

It will be realized that since its inception as an entity in Josiah I's time, active management of the firm had gone hand in hand with ownership. Modern conditions of conducting business, however, made it desirable to incorporate in 1895, particularly in view of the fact that three branches of the family were actively engaged in its direction. Therefore, the firm became Josiah Wedgwood & Sons Ltd., and the fifth generation of the family, in the persons of Cecil (1884-1916), Frank (1889-1930) and Kennard (1873-   ) took control. For some years after incorporation, the firm suffered reverses, due largely to the outbreak of the Spanish-American War which was detrimental to American business, and later to the Boer War which took two of the Directors from their duties.

Plate 82, No. 405. Jug, Queen's Ware, transfer printed Ferrara pattern in brown engraved by William Brookes in 1832; Etruria 1845. Height 6".

Plate 83, No. 439. Coffee biggin, self-colored drab body, predecessor of the drip coffee pot, Etruria 1850. Height 8".

A tile department had opened at Etruria in about 1870, but the losses which it incurred caused it to be closed in 1902; even this measure did not help the situation and various other measures of retrenchment had to be adopted. However, business revived in the course of time, and in 1902 John Goodwin became the firm's principal designer and was responsible for such popular current shapes as Edme and Patrician, while a new trend of design was developed by Alfred and Louise Powell who founded a school of free-hand painting at Etruria. In the same period Powder Blue decoration on bone china was introduced, a revival of the Chinese method of producing a stippled effect in a deep rich blue by means of a sponging technique.

After the Boer War in 1906 Kennard represented the firm in America and founded a branch office in New York. World War I had a serious effect on the industry, the lack of high-grade coal particularly affecting the quality of Etruria's products. Cecil Wedgwood, who had become the first Lord

Plate 84, No. 433. Dolphin candlestick, blue and green majolica glaze on red and yellow base, Etruria 1860. Height 9¼".

Mayor of Stoke-on-Trent, a federation of the six towns of the Potteries, unfortunately lost his life while leading his regiment in France. With Kennard in America, Frank carried on the management of Etruria, and after the War a further program of expansion was undertaken. New and up-to-date decorating shops were built and tunnel firing was introduced to replace the old coal-fired, intermittent ovens. A new designer, Daisy Makeig-Jones, was employed in addition to John Goodwin who introduced china decorations known as Fairyland lustre as well as new dinnerware designs.

Four members of the tenth generation joined the firm at this stage: Hensleigh in 1927; Josiah, son of Lord Wedgwood of Barlaston, for many years Member of Parliament for Newcastle-under-Lyme, in 1928; Tom, son of Frank, in 1928; and John in 1930. The year 1930 was a memorable one because it was the bicentennial anniversary of the birth of Josiah I. For a week the city was "en fete" and the celebrations were attended by notables from many parts of the world who came to pay tribute to the great Josiah. A pageant depicting the history of the district was put on by operatives from the whole industry, the part portraying the "Life and Times of Josiah Wedgwood" being undertaken by members of the family and 700 of the Etruria workers under the direction of Hensleigh. Exhibitions were held, public dinners arranged and the Ceramic Society sponsored a special series of meetings in tribute to "the greatest potter the world has ever known."

In the same year the firm was unfortunate enough to lose Frank, who died after his return from the Brussels Exhibition in which the firm took part. He was succeeded as Managing Director by Josiah, who has directed the firm to the present time. In 1931 Hensleigh came to America as vice-president of the New York branch, Tom took over management of production and John directed sales.

In 1933 Keith Murray, R.D.I., started to design for the company and produced a range of new and contemporary shapes which were admirably translated into the old black basalt, the new bronze basalt and the new moonstone glaze, a matt-white surface of considerable beauty. In 1935 John Goodwin retired, and the art directorship was assumed by Victor Skellern, A.R.C.A.

Plate 85, No. 360A. Teapot and cover, drab body, applied blue ornament, Etruria 1830. Height 4".

Plate 86, No. 200. Vase, black
and white jasper, presented to
H.M. Queen Mary on her visit to
Etruria, July 27, 1939. Height 8″.

An important exhibition was held at the Grafton Galleries in London in
1936 at which the work of these two men was given some prominence, as well
as that of Eric Ravilious who started designing for the company in 1937. This
exhibition introduced moonstone to the public and also showed for the first
time the new Alpine pink. Other new designs were introduced by Millicent
Taplin, also a resident artist at Etruria, who carried on the traditions of the
Powells as head of the free-hand painting department. Many of Miss Taplin's
floral patterns, several incorporating the use of silver lustre, are current
favorites.

76

THE BARLASTON PERIOD

The period of rapid artistic and technical progress since World War I culminated in 1936 when the Directors came to a decision, the importance of which had not been equalled since the founding of Etruria. Etruria as a monument to the genius of Josiah I was the latest in up-to-date planning when it first opened in 1769, but by 1936 it had obviously outlived its usefulness. The 18th century workshops, courtyards, and the old mill with square oaken shafting, while interesting historically were not suitable for modern business. Furthermore, considerable subsidence of the area had occurred, owing to coal mining operations beneath the site. As a result of an expensive and long-drawn out lawsuit in 1895, the Duchy of Lancaster, owner of the mineral rights, was restrained from further mining; nevertheless further settling caused continual trouble and expense in repairing and strengthening the buildings.

It was therefore decided, though with much regret, to abandon Etruria for new quarters. The example set one hundred and fifty years earlier by

Plate 87, No. 399. Sauce tureen, bone china, decorated by Herbert Chollerton, gold print with seal of the United States. Part of service ordered by Theodore Roosevelt for the White House in 1912. Height 5¾".

Josiah I in building the most modern plant he could devise, away from the overcrowded town in which he had previously carried on his business, was followed by his descendants. To found a new plant, Wedgwood, in 1937, bought an estate of 380 acres in the hamlet of Barlaston, the home for several generations of members of the family. Barlaston Park is a pleasant wooded tract of land with open meadows and streams, away from the smoke and grime of the city, where the new works has already been half-finished and where a model village for the employees has been started. Keith Murray, previously mentioned as one of the firm's designers, and his partner C. S. White, F.R.I.B.A., were appointed architects for the factory, while Louis de Soissons, A.R.A., F.R.I.B.A., has drawn plans for the village.

The foundation stone of this extensive enterprise was laid in 1938, with eight of the company's veteran workers taking part in the ceremonies. The Queen's Ware section of the new factory was completed in 1940, but the outbreak of World War II put an end to further construction so that Etruria is still in operation for the making of bone china. The building of the village was also brought to a halt at the outbreak of hostilities, after the completion of about ten houses.

Plate 88, No. 529. Mug, Queen's Ware, decoration in yellow, gray and black, designed by Eric Ravillious, to commemorate opening of Barlaston, 1940. Height 3⅞".

The layout of the new factory has been carefully planned with each process provided for in sequence to minimize unnecessary handling. The shops are well lighted, working conditions comfortable and every modern convenience provided for the health and pleasure of the workers. A large canteen serves inexpensive meals and provides space for concerts and dances; playing fields have been laid out and a fishing club, beekeeping club and similar outside interests are encouraged.

Plate 89, No. 513. Sculpture, terra cotta, *Beatrice,* modeled by Arnold Machin, designed so that the flame of the kiln darkens the highest parts giving color to the design. Barlaston, 1944. Height 2′ 6″.

Plate 90, No. 512. Coffee cup and saucer, bone china, Persian Pony design, red and white decoration, designed by Victor Skellern, Barlaston 1940. Height of cup 2⅜". Diameter of saucer 4¾".

The parallel between this endeavor and that of the original Etruria is further illustrated by the advances made in firing. As in Josiah's time, the latest techniques are now employed. In order to avoid the smoke and dirt attendant upon coal firing, Wedgwood is pioneering in the use of electricity for heating the biscuit and glost tunnel ovens. But while modern mechanical refinements have been incorporated in the manufacturing process, most of the work is still done by hand to maintain the character and quality of the products. The management has not lost sight of the fact that in the final analysis, it is the hand of the potter that counts.

The outbreak of World War II brought many changes in the industry. In the beginning dollar credits were of prime importance, and export business to the "hard currency" countries was therefore encouraged. For some years prior to the war, due largely to the efforts of the New York branch, a high percentage of the firm's total output went to the Americas, and this

Plate 91, No. 502. Bowl, Queen's Ware, black mat glaze, canary yellow interior, designed by Norman Wilson, Barlaston 1947. Height 2⅝".

increased during the war as the export drive was intensified. Many of the smaller potteries in the district were forcibly closed in order to supply additional labor to the export firms. With the introduction of Lend-Lease, however, the extreme urgency for dollars was somewhat lessened, while the need for workers in essential or munitions industries and for the armed services increased. Workers were drafted therefore from non-essential industries, such as pottery, and approximately two-thirds were directed into other fields. Certain raw materials became scarce and prices began to rise. This resulted in a decrease of production, while at the same time there was a demand out of all proportion to the supply. Many executives and workers, including John in England, Hensleigh in America, and Norman Wilson, Director in charge of Production at Barlaston, joined the armed services. As soon as the war was over in Europe, building was resumed at Barlaston but, while much

Plate 92, No. 528. Jug, Queen's Ware, designed by Keith Murray, Etruria 1936. Height 8¼".

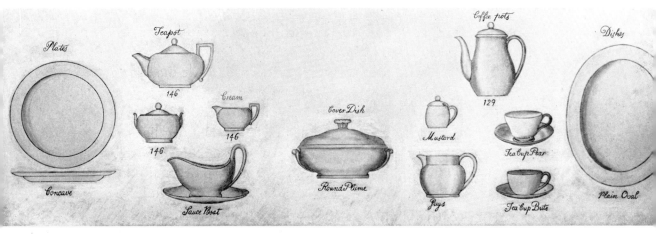

Plate 93. Shapes from Josiah Wedgwood's First Catalogue, 1770. The famous "146" teapot, "129" coffee pot, "Concave" plate and "Pear" tea cup, and many other shapes have been constantly used through 178 years and are still good today because the shapes are functional — lids fit, spouts pour and handles are comfortable to the hand.

progress has been made, there still remain (1948) several years of construction before the Barlaston plant will be completed.

Several new artists have been added within the last few years, Richard Garbe, Edward Bawden, A.R.A., Norman Wilson, who has produced some most unusual glazes, and Arnold Machin, A.R.A., some of whose work was shown by the Royal Academy at last year's exhibition.

Therefore, the "Living Tradition" of Wedgwood continues in the production of traditional shapes and patterns, as valid now as in the time of Josiah I, and also in a constant effort to produce the finest in contemporary wares.

Wedgwood has made a great contribution not only to the development of ceramic art but also through the years has been outstanding in combining art with industry. This principle was set forth by Josiah I in the introduction to his catalogue of 1787:

"The progress of the arts, at all times and in every country, depends chiefly upon the encouragement they receive from those who by their rank and affluence are legislators in taste, and who alone are capable of bestowing rewards upon the labors of industry, and the exertions of genius. It is their influence that forms the character of every age; they can turn the currents of human pursuits at their pleasure and be surrounded with either beauty or deformity . . . no art ever was or can be carried to great perfection with feeble efforts or at a small expense . . . "

82

TRADE MARKS

wedgwood   Probably the first mark. Supposed to have been used by Josiah Wedgwood at Burslem 1759-1769.

WEDGWOOD   This is a very rare mark used at the Bell Works 1764-1769.

WEDGWOOD
Wedgwood   Used in varying sizes from 1759-1769.

The circular stamp, without the inner and outer rings, and without the word Etruria is doubtless the earliest form of the Wedgwood and Bentley stamp, 1769.

This mark, with the word Etruria, was fixed in the corner, inside the plinth of old basalt vases. It is sometimes found on the pedestal of a bust or large figure. 1769-1780.

This circular stamp, with an inner and outer line, was always placed around the screw of the basalt, granite and Etruscan vases, but is never found on jasper vases. 1769-1780.

Unique script mark, Wedgwood & Bentley, 1769-1780.

Wedgwood
& Bentley
356   Mark used on Wedgwood & Bentley intaglios, with the catalogue number varying in size, 1769-1780.

W. & B.   Very small intaglios were sometimes marked W&B with the catalogue number, or simply with the number only, 1769-1780.

Wedgwood & Bentley: Etruria   1769-1780.

Rare mark found only on chocolate and white seal intaglios, usually portraits made of two layers of clay with the edges polished for mounting, 1769-1780.

WEDGWOOD
& BENTLEY

Wedgwood
& Bentley   These marks, varying in size are found upon busts, granite and basalt vases, figures, plaques, medallions and cameos, from the largest tablet to the smallest cameo. 1769-1780.

<table>
<tr><td>
Wedgwood
Wedgwood
WEDGWOOD
WEDGWOOD
</td><td>
Varying in size these marks are attributed to the period after Bentley's death (1780) and probably used for a time after Josiah's death (1795).
</td></tr>
</table>

WEDGWOOD & SONS

Very rare mark used for a short period in 1790.

JOSIAH WEDGWOOD
Feb 2 1805

Mark of Josiah Wedgwood II. Supposed to be some new partnership or change in the firm. It is found only on some basalt tripod incense burners. It may be the date when the design was first registered, 1805. Sometimes, instead of "Feb 2", the date appears as "2nd Feby."

WEDGWOOD

The mark upon the bone china or porcelain, made 1812-1815, always printed either in red, blue or in gold.

WEDGWOOD
WEDGWOOD

From 1769 to the present day this mark has been impressed in the clay on Queen's Ware, or printed in color. In recent times the words Etruria and Barlaston and the name of the pattern have in many cases been printed in addition to the trade mark. From 1780, ornamental jasper, black basalt, cane, terra cotta and Queen's Ware are always marked with this stamp. The name "England" was added in 1891.

WEDGWOOD
ETRURIA
WEDGWOOD
ETRURIA
Wedgwood
Etruria

These marks are rarely found on pieces of a very high character. Adopted about 1840 but used for only a short period.

WEDGWOOD

This mark now in use on china was adopted in 1878 when the manufacture of bone china was revived. It is printed in various colors.

ENGLAND

England was added to the mark Wedgwood in 1891 to comply with the American Customs Regulation known as the McKinley Tariff Act.

WEDGWOOD
BONE CHINA
MADE IN
ENGLAND

Mark used today on bone china, developed from mark of 1878.

OF ETRURIA
WEDGWOOD
MADE IN
ENGLAND
BARLASTON

This mark, printed in color, is being used today on Queen's Ware, starting in 1940.

84

DATE MARKS ON EARTHENWARE

In 1860 Wedgwood introduced a system of date marking in addition to the trade mark. These date marks consisted of three capital letters: the first indicating the month, the second being the potter's mark and the third the year in which the piece was made.

The monthly marks from 1860 to 1864 are as follows:

January	J	April	A	July	V	October	O
February	F	May	Y	August	W	November	N
March	M	June	T	September	S	December	D

From 1864 to 1907 these monthly marks were changed to the following:

January	J	April	A	July	L	October	O
February	F	May	M	August	W	November	N
March	R	June	T	September	S	December	D

The yearly marks from 1860 to 1930 ran in three cycles beginning with the letter O for 1860 and continuing through the alphabet in sequence to Z for 1871.

A second cycle began with A for 1872 and went to Z for 1897.

A third cycle started with A for 1898 to Z for 1923.

During this third cycle (in 1907) a figure indicating the cycle was substituted for the letter denoting the month since up to this point it was difficult to determine whether a piece was made in the first, second or third cycle without consulting pattern or shape books or by other circumstantial evidence, as the following example points out:

Month	Potter	Year		
V	X	O	July 1860	(the beginning of date marking first cycle)
L	X	S	July 1864	(at the change of the code letter for months)
L	X	S	July 1890	(note the second cycle appears the same as the first)
Cycle				
3	X	J	1907	(a number denoting the cycle substituted for monthly mark)
3	X	S	1916	(1916 being the year S in the third cycle)

This confusing system of dating was discontinued in 1930. From that date a number designates the month in chronological sequence. A letter gives the potter's mark and the last two numbers give the actual year. For example:

Month	Potter	Year	
7	X	30	July 1930
7	X	32	July 1932
7	X	47	July 1947

X has been used to indicate the potter throughout this explanation. There have been many potters with their letters changing from time to time and assigned to others at the end of their term of service.

REGISTRY MARKS

From 1842 to 1883 when the British Patent Office employed a Registry mark on English manufactured goods, Wedgwood used the mark in addition to the trade mark along with other manufacturers which indicated that the design was registered in the British Patent Office. When this mark appears it is possible to tell the exact year, month and date of an object by using the following table.

INDEX TO THE LETTERS FOR EACH MONTH AND YEAR FROM 1842 TO 1867

Year		Month	
1842	X	January	C
1843	H	February	G
1844	C	March, 1845	W
1845	A	April	H
1846	I	May	E
1847	F	June	M
1848	U	July	I
1849	S	August	R
1850	V	September	D
1851	P	October	B
1852	D	November	K
1853	Y	December	A
1854	J		
1855	E		
1856	L		
1857	K		
1858	B		
1859	M		
1860	Z		
1861	R		
1862	O		
1863	G		
1864	N		
1865	W		
1866	Q		
1867	T		

CLASS
YEAR
MONTH R^d DAY
PARCEL

MAY 23, 1842

Letter R used from 1st to 19th September, 1857

December, 1860, Letter K used.

YEAR		MONTH	
1868	X	January	C
1869	H	February	G
1870	C	March	W
1871	A	April	H
1872	I	May	E
1873	F	June	M
1874	U	July	I
1875	S	August	R
1876	V	September	D
1877	P	October	B
1878	D	November	K
1879	Y	December	A
1880	J		
1881	E		
1882	L		
1883	K		

WEDGWOOD WORKS OR FACTORIES

CHURCHYARD WORKS	. . . .	1649 - 1749	*Burslem*

CLIFF BANK WORKS . . . . 1753 - 1754 *Stoke*
Josiah's partnership with John Harrison

FENTON LOW . . . . 1754 - 1759 *Fenton*
Partnership with Thomas Whieldon

IVY HOUSE . . . . 1759 - 1763 *Burslem*

BRICK HOUSE or BELL WORKS . . . . . 1763 - 1769 *Burslem*

ETRURIA . . . . 1769 - 1940 *Etruria*

BARLASTON . . . . 1940 - *Barlaston*

87

WEDGWOOD ARTISTS

MODELERS AT ETRURIA

Artist's Name and Working Period

Arnold Austin (also at Barlaston), 1904-1947
J. A. Austin, 1904-1927
William Beattie, 1856-1864
William Bedson, 1773-1776
John Billington, 1789-?
Joseph Birks, 1867-1875
Simon Birks, 1867-1875
Thomas Boot, 1769-1773
Henry Brownsword, 1849-1853
Charles Denby, 1769-1770
Thomas Greatbach, 1844-1864
William Greatbach (also at Burslem), 1763-?

William Hackwood, 1769-1832
William Keeling, 1769-?
Edward Keys, 1845-1853
Eric Owen (at Barlaston), 1947-
Frederick Schenck, 1872-1873
William Theed, 1799-1814
Henry Till, 1881-1883
Charles Toft, 1880-1889
John Voyez, 1768-1769
Edward Watson, 1768-1769
Henry Webber, 1784-1801
William Wood (also at Burslem), 1767-1808

MODELERS IN ROME

Angelo Dalmazzoni, 1788-1792
John Flaxman, R.A., 1775-1800
Micheli Angielo Mangiarotti, 1788

Camillo Pacetti, 1787
John de Vaere, 1787-1798

MODELERS WHO HAVE EXECUTED COMMISSIONS

John Bacon, 1769-1777
Mr. Birch, 1779-1791
John Coward, 1765-1769
John Dassier, 1770
Mr. De Wilde, 1777
J. A. Hammersley, 1844-1845
John Charles Lochee, 1774-1788
E. G. Mountstephen, 1788-1792
Charles Peart, 1788-1794

Mr. Pezey, 1776
Hugus Protat, 1870-1871
Jessie M. Riding, 1919
Joachim Smith, 1774-1782
P. Stephan, 1774
George Stubbs, 1780-1790
James Tassie, 1769-1791
E. W. Wyon, 1852-1866

SUPPLIERS OF PLASTER CASTS

John Cheese, 1769
John Flaxman, Sr., 1781-1788
Oliver and Grant Hoskins, 1769-1779

Mary Landre, 1769-1774
Theodore and Richard Parker, 1769-1774

FULL TIME DESIGNERS AND ART DIRECTORS

Thomas Allen, 1880-1900
John E. Goodwin, 1904-1934
Emile Lessore, 1859-1875

Victor Skellern, A.R.C.A., F.S.I.A., N.R.D.,
   1923-
Millicent Taplin, M.S.I.A., N.R.D., 1927-

88

DESIGNERS WHO HAVE EXECUTED COMMISSIONS

Lady Diana Beauclerc, 1789
Walter Crane, 1867-1877
Arnold Machin, A.R.A., A.R.C.A., 1938-
Eric Ravillious, A.R.C.A., 1935-1943
Sir Joshua Reynolds, P.R.A., 1778

John Skeaping, 1930
Lady Templetown, 1783-1787
Star Wedgwood, 1930-
Anna Zinkeisen, 1930

DESIGNERS AND ART ADVISERS

Sir Charles Holmes, 1930
Keith Murray, 1932-
Alfred and Louise Powell, 1910-

Norman Wilson (Present Production Director), 1927-

ENGRAVERS

Mr. Baddeley, 1852-1877
William Blake (Catalogue illustrations), 1815
Semi Bourne, 1813
William Brookes, 1811-1839
E. Davies, 1903-1932
Samuel Doncaster, 1806-1811
William Downing, 1806-1811
G. Ford, 1842-1843
Louis Hackwood, 1799
William Hales, 1806-1808
J. Heath, 1840-1877
Mr. Hordley, 1824-1847
Jesse Hulme, 1842-1844

Paul Hulme, 1919-
Thomas Longmore, 1809-1810
J. Mollart, 1806-1811
Mr. Pepper, 1839-1865
Thomas Robinson, 1806-1810
Robert Ryles, 1816-1852
Sadler & Green, 1764-1791
Mr. Sherwin, 1860-1864
T. Sparkes, 1812-1832
A. Toft, 1842-1843
W. Wareham, 1860-1874
John Taylor Wedgwood (Catalogue illustrations), circa. 1804-1817

ARTISTS AND PAINTERS

Herbert A. Cholerton, 1901-
James Hodgkiss, circa. 1900-1925
Arthur Dale Holland, 1908-1940
David Rhodes, 1769-1776

Aaron Steel, 1784-1812
Ralph Wilcox, 1769-1776
Sarah Wilcox, 1769-1776

* These lists were compiled by the Wedgwood Museum and include only those artists who have made major contributions.

GLOSSARY

AGATE • Pottery made to imitate agate stone by wedging tinted clays together so that the colors extend through the body. See *Variegated Wares*.

ALPINE PINK • Self-colored pink translucent bone china. It is made in traditional Wedgwood shapes and includes a dessert service in the well-known Nautilus shape. Introduced in 1936.

BALL CLAY • Dark-colored clay, which becomes lighter in firing, quarried mainly in Dorset, England but found in other parts of the world. Used to give plasticity and strength to the pottery body.

BAMBOO WARE • Dark shade of Cane ware made to imitate bamboo. Introduced by Wedgwood 1770. See *Cane*.

BARBERINI VASE • See *Portland Vase*.

BAS-RELIEF • See *Jasper*.

BISCUIT • Pottery or porcelain which has been fired once but not glazed. Same as bisque.

BISQUE • See *Biscuit*.

BLACK BASALT • Fine grained, unglazed, black stoneware, refinement of the earlier Egyptian black, made by staining the body with manganese dioxide. The various improvements made in the body by Wedgwood gave it a richer hue, finer grain and smoother surface. Perfected about 1770, it was the first ornamental ware developed by Josiah Wedgwood. He used it for both useful and ornamental wares. A large group of relief plaques, vases, busts, medallions, portraits, seals and small intaglios were made in black basalt. It formed also the ground on which Wedgwood executed classical encaustic paintings with a special palette of enamel colors that gave a mat surface though unglazed when fired, and produced a similar effect to that of the old Greek and Etruscan vases. Relief ornamentation of black basalt started in the jasper period of 1774 and has been carried on ever since using models created by Flaxman, Hackwood, Stubbs and others.

BLUNGER • Vat with mechanical stirrers for mixing clay.

BODY • Name given to the composite materials of which potter's clay is made. The term body is generally used when referring to earthenware or stoneware body. The term paste is used almost exclusively when referring to porcelain or china.

BONE ASH • Calcined ox bones crushed and ground to a powder, and used as the main ingredient in bone china.

BONE CHINA • Soft paste body made from china stone and china clay with a large percentage of calcined bone added to give it whiteness and translucency. In 1812 bone china was manufactured by Wedgwood but was discontinued in 1816 owing to the enormous demand for Queen's Ware. It was resumed in 1878.

BUFF WARE • See *Dry Bodies*.

CAMEO • Ornaments in relief as distinguished from intaglio. Specifically, that which is in one color on a ground of a different color. Used here to refer to those in jasper or other bodies made by Wedgwood.

CANE WARE • Tan-colored stoneware. In 1770 Wedgwood refined the clays used by peasant potters for their buff brown wares into a new and lighter body which he called "Cane." See *Dry Bodies, Colored Bodies*.

CASTING • See *Processes*.

CAULIFLOWER WARE • Cream ware modeled and colored in imitation of a cauliflower, developed during Josiah Wedgwood's partnership with Whieldon, 1759. See *Green Glaze*.

C. C. WARE • An abbreviation for Cream Color Ware.

CELADON • French name given originally to a glaze on Chinese porcelain. In 1805, Wedgwood applied the term to a self-colored earthenware body of a sea-green color. See *Colored Bodies*.

90

CHINA CLAY OR KAOLIN • Whitest clay known, found in England in Devon and Cornwall as well as other parts of the world, produced by the decomposition of granitic rocks over a long period of time.

CHINA STONE • Known also as Cornish stone. Similar to china clay but at an earlier stage of decomposition. When fired at a high temperature it becomes a hard opaque glass.

CHAMPAGNE • See *Colored Bodies*.

CHOCOLATE • See *Colored Bodies*.

CLAY • A stiff viscous earth, found in many varieties near the surface of the ground or at various depths. It forms with water a tenacious paste, capable of being molded into any shape. See *Body*.

COLORED BODIES • Self-colored body obtained by use of coloring oxides or ocherous earths. The early successes of Wedgwood's dry Cane ware encouraged further research and the development of other colored clays. In 1805 Wedgwood introduced Celadon. Followed in 1850 by Lavender Blue and in 1930 by Champagne. These self-colored bodies were, apart from bone china, the most important technical and artistic development by Wedgwood in the 19th century.

COMBED WARE • Pottery with a surface decoration produced by combing the wet, newly applied slip on the surface of pottery with a coarse comb or wire brush in a wavy or zigzag pattern. This form of decoration was developed in 1760 into its highest form by Josiah Wedgwood. See *Variegated Wares*.

CREAM COLOR WARE • Name by which Wedgwood's Queen's Ware was first known before he became "Potter to the Queen." See *Queen's Ware*.

DIPPING • See *Processes*.

DRAB BODIES • See *Dry Bodies*.

DRY BODIES • Non-porous stoneware body requiring no glaze. Made basically from local marls with additions of coloring oxides or ocherous earths to give the right hue. The dry bodies include basalt, jasper, rosso antico, cane, buff, drab, chocolate and olive. They were made in a variety of shapes, both useful and ornamental, such as jugs, teapots, bough pots, vases, inkstands, lamps, busts and portrait medallions.

DUSTING • Application of a glaze preparation in the form of powder to the surface of the body and afterwards melted in the kiln. See *Glaze*.

EARTHENWARE • Opaque ware which is porous after the first firing, and which must be glazed before it can be applied to domestic use.

EGYPTIAN BLACK • See *Basalt*.

ENAMELING • See *Processes*.

ENCAUSTIC DECORATION • Painting by means of a special palette of colors mixed with wax which is afterwards fused to the ware. It was done mainly in red and white on black basalt, by Josiah Wedgwood in imitation of the early Etruscan ware. See *Black Basalt, Etruscan Ware*.

ENGINE TURNING LATHE • A lathe, equipped with an eccentric motion, built for Josiah Wedgwood by Matthew Boulton about 1763. By means of this lathe geometric, diced and fluted decorations were incised on vases and other such pieces.

ENGRAVING • See *Processes*.

ETRUSCAN WARE • Black ware with encaustic painting mainly in red and white. The name was derived from ancient Etruria.

FAIRYLAND LUSTRE • See *Lustre*.

FETTLING • See *Processes*.

FILTER PRESS • Series of canvas bags supported in frames bolted together, into which slip is pumped under pressure. Water is squeezed out of the slip, leaving a cake of plastic clay in the bag.

FIRING • See *Processes*.

FLINT • Pure silica, the natural stone. It is calcined in kilns and ground to a fine powder. Flint imparts strength and solidity to the body and prevents warping.

GLAZE • Glassy preparation applied to the surface of biscuit ware to render it impervious to liquids.

Green Glaze • A glaze applied to shapes and decorations in various shades of green. From 1754 to 1759 Josiah Wedgwood developed the green glaze ware, to produce a new species of colored ware to be fired along with the Variegated wares in the common glost oven. Green glaze was Experiment No. 7 in Josiah Wedgwood's "Experiment Book" started in 1759. Since then green glaze, in many shapes, particularly wares made to resemble leaves, has been continually made.

Lead Glaze • Transparent glaze used on ceramics. It was first a powdered lead ore (smithum) which was applied to the surface by dusting and was called Galena Glaze. Later a fluid lead glaze, consisting of borax, china clay, whiting, etc., was developed and is now in common use.

Majolica Glaze • Lead glaze, stained with coloring oxides to produce brilliant color effects. It was introduced by Wedgwood in 1860 for dessert services and ornamental ware. The name Majolica derives from a type of ware made in Marjorca, Italy from the 15th century.

Matt Glaze • Dull glaze without gloss. Matt glaze was introduced by Wedgwood in 1933. The best known in this category is Moonstone. Other colors include straw, April green and grey.

Moonstone Glaze • Matt glaze introduced by Wedgwood in 1933. Its driven snow effect has been employed by Keith Murray, a Wedgwood artist, for contemporary design of both table ware and ornamental pieces.

Salt Glaze • Transparent hard glaze with pitted or orange peel surface, produced by throwing rock salt into the kiln from above, at the maximum degree of heat. When the salt volatilizes a chemical reaction takes place between the salt fumes and the silica in the clay creating a thin coating on the surface of the ware. Thomas Wedgwood achieved a considerable reputation with salt glaze made at the Churchyard Works during Josiah's apprenticeship to him, 1744-1749. Josiah's later improvements in cream-colored ware, marked the decline of the use of salt glaze.

Smear Glaze • Semi-glaze or thin deposit on the surface of pottery, produced by smearing the inside of the saggar with the glazing preparation. This vaporizes in the heat of the kiln and settles on the surface of the enclosed ware. Smear glaze was a development following salt glaze and is often mistaken for it.

GLAZING • See *Processes.*

GLOST FIRE • Firing process through which ware passes to fuse the glaze.

GRANITE WARE • Earthenware with a graying or blueish mottled glaze, made by Wedgwood in imitation of granite. (Not to be confused with granite ware made by later potters.) See *Pearl Ware, Variegated Wares.*

GREEN GLAZE WARE • See *Glaze, Green Glaze.*

GREEN FROG WARE • See *Russian Service.*

GROUNDLAYING • See *Processes.*

INTAGLIO • Sunken or incised design, the opposite of cameo. Wedgwood made a wide range of intaglios in black basalt and jasper for rings and seals during the latter part of the 18th century.

JASPER • Dense white vitrefied stoneware body of nearly the same properties as porcelain. When formed thin it is translucent. It has a fine unglazed surface. The body contains carbonate or sulphate of baryta. When colored throughout the body it is called solid jasper. When the white body is dipped in a solution of colored jasper (after 1785) it is called jasper dip or bas-relief. In 1774 after a long series of experiments, Josiah Wedgwood recorded his discovery of "A white porcelain bisque of exquisite beauty and delicacy, possessing the general qualities of the 'Basaltes' together with that of receiving colors through its whole substance, in a manner which no other body, ancient or modern, has been known to do." This body was later named jasper. Cameos, portraits, medallions, plaques, vases and many other articles were made and are still made of the jasper body, with decorations in relief. Artists and modelers were gathered from all parts of the world to create designs for this elaborate ware. The outstanding triumph in jasper was the copy of the "Barberini" or "Portland Vase." In the decoration of jasper each section of ornament is molded separately and applied by hand to the thrown and turned piece.

JASPER DIP • Colored solution applied to the white jasper body by dipping. See *Jasper*.

JOLLYING • See *Processes*.

KAOLIN • See *China Clay*.

KILN • Intermittent or tunnel oven in which ware is fired. Intermittent or bottle kilns are fired by coal. The ware is placed in saggars to protect it from the flames and fumes during firing. In tunnel kilns, fired by oil, gas or electricity, the ware moves through continuously on trucks.

LATHE • Machine on which ware is held and rotated to produce an even surface.

LEAD GLAZE • See *Glaze*.

LUSTRE • Iridescent or metallic film on the surface of ware obtained by the use of metallic oxides, gold, silver, copper, etc. Introduced by Wedgwood in 1805. The metallic oxides are suspended in an oily medium in which form it is painted on ware. To obtain a more complicated decoration than could be created by simple painting, the resist method of application was introduced. By this method intricate designs are painted or printed on ware with a resist material such as china clay mixed with honey or syrup. The lustre is then applied over the entire piece and fired or fused to the ware. It will not adhere to the portion protected by the resist which retains the color of the body. This type of decoration became popular in England in the early 19th century following the discovery of platinum in 1796, and has been used extensively on modern dinnerware, both earthenware and china. Wedgwood's designers, Alfred and Louise Powell, Victor Skellern and Millicent Taplin, combined lustre with colors in free-hand painting. The metallic decoration of the 18th century, which has been termed silver and gold lustre, is not a true lustre process as known today since the metal was applied as a pigment with a brush.

Fairyland Lustre • Type of decoration used in ornamental china pieces, showing whimsical creatures in fairyland settings designed by Daisy Makeig-Jones and introduced in 1924.

Moonlight Lustre • Purple and gold lustre used by Wedgwood as early as 1805.

MAJOLICA • See *Glaze*.

MARBLED WARE • Earthenware made to imitate marble. The effect was obtained by laying on lines and splashes of different colored slips which were sponged or combed together. See *Variegated Wares*.

MARL • Amorphous deposits of lime, sand and clay.

MATT GLAZE • See *Glaze*.

MELON WARE • Ware modeled and colored in imitation of a melon. Made by Whieldon, Wedgwood and other English potters in the latter part of the 18th century.

MODELING • See *Processes*.

MOLD MAKING • See *Processes*.

MOONLIGHT LUSTRE • See *Lustre*.

MOONSTONE GLAZE • See *Glaze*.

MORTAR WARE • Extremely hard vitreous stoneware body introduced by Wedgwood prior to 1789 for the making of mortars, pestles and chemical ware. It resists the strongest acids and corrosives and makes what are still considered to be the best mortars obtainable.

MUFFLE • Fireclay box or interior of a kiln to which flames have no access.

NAUTILUS WARE • Ware made to imitate the Nautilus shell. The first catalogue of Josiah Wedgwood's shapes compiled in the latter part of the 18th century illustrates the Nautilus shell dessert service composed of center bowl, cream bowl and plates. Nautilus is made in Queen's Ware, Alpine Pink, Bone China and Moonstone.

OLIVE • See *Dry Bodies.*

ORNAMENTAL WARES • Josiah Wedgwood divided his wares into two main classifications, ornamental and useful. Ornamental wares were further subdivided into the following 20 classes: 1. Intaglios and medallions or cameos; 2. Bas-reliefs, medallions, tablets, etc.; 3. Medallions, etc. of Kings, Queens and illustrious persons of Asia, Egypt and Greece (100); 4. Ancient Roman History subjects (60 medallions); 5. Heads of Illustrious Romans (40); 6. The 12 Caesars and their Empresses; 7. Series of emperors, Nerva to Constantine the Great (52); 8. Heads of the popes (253); 9. Kings and Queens of England and France (100); 10. Heads of illustrious moderns (230); 11. Busts and statuettes of boys, animals and distinguished persons (142); 12. Lamps and candelabra; 13. Tea and coffee services; 14. Flower pots and root pots; 15. Ornamental vases in terra cotta; 16. Antique vases of black basalt with relief ornaments; 17. Vases, tablets, etc. with encaustic painting; 18. Vases and tripods in Jasper; 19. Inkstands, paint chests, eye cups, mortars; 20. Thermometers for measuring strong fire.

ORNAMENTING • See *Processes.*

PARIAN • Hard paste porcelain produced by the casting process. Parian was used extensively by 19th century potters for making statuettes and busts in imitation of Parian marble. Wedgwood first used it in 1860 but never to any great extent. Biblical statuary is an example of Wedgwood's application of Parian.

PASTE • See *Body.*

PEARL WARE • White earthenware body containing a greater percentage of flint and white clay than cream-colored earthenware. A small amount of cobalt is added to the glaze for a still further whitening effect. Pearl was first made by Josiah Wedgwood in 1779 but never extensively used. It is important as the precursor of a granite ware later made by other potters. (Not to be confused with Wedgwood's granite ware made to imitate the granite stone under the classification of *Variegated Wares*.)

PESTLES • See *Mortar Ware.*

PIE CRUST • Unglazed cane ware made in imitation of pie crust in the early 19th century to substitute for pie crust in times of a flour shortage. An example is the famous "Game Pie Dish." See *Cane.*

PORCELAIN • Translucent vitrified ware which has been fired at a high temperature.

PORTLAND VASE • The most famous of Josiah Wedgwood's reproductions is his copy of the Portland Vase. The original, an example of Graeco-Roman work in glass, is the sepulchral urn which contained the ashes of the Roman Emperor Alexander Severus, and his mother Mammaea, which was buried about 235 A.D. and was dug up by order of Pope Barberini, between 1623-44. It was bought by Sir William Hamilton in 1782, sold to the Duchess of Portland in 1785 and after her death in 1786 was lent to Josiah Wedgwood so that he might reproduce it. After four years of experiment to get the correct color, surface and texture the copy was completed. This vase is also known as the "Barberini Vase."

POT BANK • A works, pottery, factory or place where clay products are made.

POTTERY • Soft, lightly fired, opaque earthenware.

POWDER BLUE • Blue speckled ground color used during the K'ang-hsi period and later reigns in China. Wedgwood was the first English potter to discover how to revive this method of decoration for use on bone china in the 20th century. The effect is obtained by painting on a layer of wet color and stippling with a fine grained sponge.

PRINTING • See *Processes.*

PROCESSES

Casting • Process of forming shapes by pouring slip into dry plaster molds which immediately absorb moisture from the slip. When a sufficient thickness of clay has adhered to the inside of the mold the remaining slip is poured out and the mold set to dry, after which the form is removed from the mold.

Notches in one part of the mold lock into the other insuring a close fit. In drying, the clay piece contracts allowing removal from the mold. The cast article must be carefully cleaned and seams smoothed. Working molds consist of two or more parts to facilitate removal of casting after drying.

Dipping • Process of glazing by submersion in a liquid glaze composition.

Enameling • Pigments added over a glaze and given a separate firing in the decorating kiln.

Engraving • Cutting of designs on copper plates for reproduction on ware. See *Printing*.

Fettling • Finishing of a piece of ware in the clay state by touching up and removing traces of seams, cast lines, etc.

Firing • Process of transforming clay into pottery by burning it in a special oven or kiln.

Glazing • Application of the glaze to the ware. This is done by dipping or spraying. See *Glaze*.

Groundlaying • Process of giving an even texture of color to the ware. A coating of oil is applied to the ware by a dabbing process with a fine silk boss. Color in a powder form is dusted over the oil surface with a piece of cotton wool and the oil is allowed to absorb as much dust as it will. The firing drives out the oil leaving the color firmly fixed to the ware.

Jiggering • Process of making plates by placing clay on a revolving mold or jigger. A bat of clay is flattened on a revolving disc or spreader. This clay is then placed on a plaster mold which forms the front of the plate. As the mold revolves on the "jigger" the profile is brought down to scrape away the excess clay leaving the exact thickness between the profile and the mold for making the plate and at the same time forming the back of the plate.

Jollying • Process of making cups. The same as jiggering except in reverse. The profile makes the inside of the cup and the mold forms the outside. See *Jiggering*.

Modeling • Process of making the original pattern or design from which the master mold is made.

Mold Making • Making of molds so that many reproductions may be made from the modeler's pattern.

From a drawn design the original clay model is produced with great accuracy and skill to preserve detail and quality of design. Allowances must be made for shrinkage from "wet clay" to "dry clay" size and again during firing process. In the next process, three molds are made from plaster of paris because of its absorptive property. The block mold is made from the original clay model. A case mold is made from the block mold, and from the case mold the potter's working mold is made from which the cast piece is produced. The working molds are reproduced from the case mold as required.

Ornamenting • Process of applying relief decoration to ware while still in the plastic state. Clay is pressed into ornamenting or "pitcher" molds forming figures, leaves, scrolls, bands and other types of relief decoration. The relief is lifted out and applied to the ware after moistening the surface of the ware with water. The ornament is fixed by the skillful pressure of the craftsmen's fingers. This method of hand-ornamenting has not altered since the days of Josiah Wedgwood. Embossed or hand-applied clay bas-reliefs are made in "pitcher" molds by a figure maker and applied by an ornamenter, after wetting the surface. The ornament is fixed by skillful pressure of the craftsman's finger; and a sensitive touch is necessary to preserve the fine detail of the applied ornament.

Overglaze Decoration • Ornamentation by painting or printing designs on the glazed surface.

Printing • Art of transferring engraved patterns to the surface of ware by means of tissue paper and prepared ink. Printing on pottery was invented by Sadler & Green of Liverpool 1755. Josiah Wedgwood bought the right to do his own printing in 1763. Printing was done in the Chelsea Studios in 1770. Wedgwood employed his own engravers to make his designs in 1780.

Throwing • Process of making ware on the potter's wheel. The name comes from the action of throwing a ball of soft clay down upon the revolving wheel. The ball is then centered on the wheel and worked up with the hands.

Turning • Process of shaping on a horizontal lathe similar to that used in the turning of wood. The "Turner" receives the ware in its "greenhard" state, places it on a "chum" (a hollow drum which holds the piece) and shaves or turns the piece to impart lightness and finish.

Underglaze Decoration • Ornamentation by painting or printing designs on the fired biscuit before it is glazed.

PUG MILL • Cylinder, either upright or horizontal, equipped with knives, similar to a food chopper on a large scale, which cuts up the clay and forces it out in a cylindrical shape, ready for potting.

QUEEN'S WARE • Earthenware of an ivory or cream color developed by Josiah Wedgwood. In 1759 Josiah Wedgwood recorded in the preface of his Experiment Book "This suite of experiments was begun about the end of 1759, in my partnership with Mr. Whieldon for the improvement of our manufacture of earthenware." For the first decade after entering business for himself in 1759 he concentrated his experiments on improving the quality and design of this cream-colored earthenware. His success was not complete until after 1768 when the Staffordshire potters learned that true china clay (kaolin) was to be found in Cornwall. The discovery of calcined flint stones to harden and whiten the body, along with the manner of using it, marks the first stage in the development of Queen's Ware. It was first composed of ball clay from Dorsetshire, calcined flint and local clays. China clay and china stone from Cornwall were added to the mixture about 1770 and the local clays were gradually dropped. The glaze invented by William Greatbach while he was working at Etruria, called "Greatbach's China Glaze" finally completed the development of cream color earthenware. This cream color earthenware came to be known as "Queen's Ware" when Josiah Wedgwood made a tea set for Queen Charlotte, wife of George III of England in 1765. This and subsequent orders pleased her sufficiently for her to allow it in the future to bear the name of "Queen's Ware." It was with this table ware that Josiah Wedgwood laid the foundation for his fame and fortune and with which he inaugurated the British pottery industry. This same cream color ware was used for the making of the famous Imperial Russian Service for Empress Catherine of Russia (Catherine the Great) in 1774. See *Russian Service*.

RED WARE • Hard fine stoneware. See *Rosso Antico*.

RELIEF ORNAMENTS • Ornaments made in molds and applied by hand. See *Jasper, Ornamenting Processes*.

RESIST • See *Lustre*.

ROCKINGHAM WARE • Brown and yellow mottled glaze on cream ware. It was used to a limited extent by Wedgwood in the 19th century.

Rosso ANTICO • Name given by Josiah Wedgwood to his red ware, which was a refinement of the earlier red ware introduced by the Elers brothers.

RUSSIAN SERVICE • Dinner service made for Catherine the Great, Empress of Russia in 1774 also known as the Imperial Russian Service and the Green Frog Service. The service contained 952 pieces, decorated with 1244 hand-painted views of English estates. Josiah Wedgwood employed a large staff of artists to complete this service.

SAGGARS • Fireclay boxes in which pottery is packed in a kiln to protect it from the direct action of the flames.

SALT GLAZE • See *Glaze*.

SELF COLORED • See *Colored Bodies*.

SILVER LUSTRE • See *Lustre*.

Slip • Potters' clay in a liquid state of about the same consistency as cream, used for slip decoration or casting.

Slip Decoration • Process of decorating pottery by applying slip over the surface in dots and lines or tracing designs with slip applied through a quill. Similar to ornamenting a cake with icing.

Smear Glaze • See *Glaze*.

Speckled Ware • See *Variegated Wares*.

Sprigged Ware • Molded relief decoration applied or sprigged directly to the body from a mold.

Sprinkled Ware • See *Variegated Ware*.

Stoneware • Opaque, vitrified, hard body fired at a high temperature, so named because of its excessive hardness, which renders it practically impervious to water without glazing. Stoneware was the principal article of manufacture at the beginning of Josiah Wedgwood's partnership with Whieldon in 1754. Thomas Wedgwood was making stoneware as early as 1710. It is the connecting link between earthenware and porcelain.

Throwing • See *Processes*.

Turning • See *Processes*.

Tortoise-shell Ware • Earthenware made to imitate the shell of a tortoise. Metallic oxides were dusted on the surface of ware: manganese to give bronze and purple, copper for green, etc. When fired the mingling of colors produced markings in variegated colors. Agate wares are colored throughout the body, while tortoise-shell color is in the glaze only. See *Variegated Wares*.

Two-Color Slip Wares • Two different colored clays used in the same article. The contrasting of different colored clays in the same piece is a well known feature of many jasper and Queen's Ware patterns. Two-color slip ware is a modern extension of this form of decoration, introduced in 1936.

Useful Wares • Josiah Wedgwood divided his wares into two main classifications, useful and ornamental. Useful Wares are those to be used in the service of food as contrasted with those of a purely ornamental character.

Variegated Wares • Earthenwares made by the use of different colored clays extending throughout the body as in agate ware or by the mixture of colors in the slip glazes as in mottled, sprinkled, freckled, marbled and tortoise-shell wares.

Vitreous Body • A body converted to a glass-like substance by fusion at high temperature.

CATALOGUE*

EARLY WARE-TRIALS AND MOLDS

1a. Posset pot, slip ware, yellow and brown, 1700. Hgt. 4″.

1b. Jug, red ware, engine turned, Etruria 1769. Hgt. 3″.

1c. Model, salt glaze, Burslem 1767. Hgt. 2½″.

1d. Teapot, red ware, unglazed, crabstock handle and spout, mid-eighteenth century. Hgt. 2½″.

1e. Trials, tray of 56 trials in the development of Queen's Ware Burslem 1759.

1f. Vase, black basalt, engine lathe turned, applied festoons, Etruria 1770. Hgt. 5¼″.

1g. Two trial teapots, Egyptian black, excessive firing caused the two teapots to adhere, Whieldon-Wedgwood 1756. Hgt. 7″.

1h. Three molds for sprigging, Whieldon-Wedgwood 1757. Hgt. 2″.

1i. Teapot, red ware, sprigged *Imp and Arabesque* pattern, Whieldon-Wedgwood 1759. Hgt. 3″.

1j. Two fragments, red ware, *Imp and Arabesque* decoration, at Whieldon-Wedgwood factory site, 1757. Hgt. 3″.

1k. Two fragments, earthenware, tortoiseshell glaze, showing improvement in the body after the use of flint was introduced, a forerunner of Queen's Ware, 1758. Hgt. 1″.

1m. Plate, cream color, signed by Enoch Wood 1826. The history of the plate inscribed on its surface reads in part, "This dish was made the first year after Wedgwood and Bentley moved from Burslem to Etruria," Etruria 1770. Dia. 16″.

WHIELDON-WEDGWOOD PERIOD

1. Teapot, marbled, red and black, thrown and turned, Whieldon 1752. Hgt. 5″. Excavated at Whieldon factory site in 1925.

2. Cream jug, marbled, unglazed, thrown and turned, handle rolled and grafted into body, Whieldon 1752. Hgt. 3½″.

3. Teapot, marbled with splashes of on-glaze colors, thrown and turned, rolled handle, found at Whieldon factory site, Whieldon-Wedgwood 1755. Hgt. 4½″.

4. Teapot, marbled, thrown and turned with rolled handle and line of white slip applied to the cover, found at Whieldon factory site, Whieldon-Wedgwood 1755. Hgt. 3½″.

5. Mug, marbled, thrown and turned, strip handle, found hanging by handle at Whieldon factory site, Whieldon-Wedgwood 1756. Hgt. 4″.

6. Beer mug, marbled, thrown and turned, strip handle, lead glaze, found at Whieldon factory site submerged in mud, no trace of decomposition, Whieldon-Wedgwood 1754. Hgt. 5″.

7. Teapot, red ware, sprigged with cream color, *Royal Coat of Arms — a Lion, Unicorn,* etc., first effort at applied ornamentation. 1752. Dia. 3¾″.

8. Saucer, marbled, red and black, white slip line decoration on edge, Whieldon 1752. Dia. 4″.

9. Teapot cover, marbled, unglazed, red and black, white applied ornament and slip line decoration, sponge finish, "slurry," found at Whieldon factory site, Whieldon 1756. Hgt. 1½″.

10. Knife, marbled handle, galena glaze red

---

* In this catalogue, objects are numbered consecutively. However, certain numbers are skipped as all the objects brought from England for this exhibition could not be shown due to limited exhibition space.

and white, found at Whieldon factory site. Whieldon-Wedgwood 1757. Length 11″.

11. Knife, marbled, cream, red and black, later development of marbling with more detailed pattern, Burslem 1762. Length 11″.

12. Fork, marbled, cream, red, black, Burslem 1762. Length 11″.

13. Knife, marbled, Burslem 1762. Length 11″.

14. Knife haft, marbled, molded with fluted decoration, found at Whieldon factory site, Whieldon-Wedgwood 1756. Length 3¼″.

15. Knife haft, inlaid marbling on red body, found at Whieldon factory site badly blistered due to fire, polished off, redipped in glaze and fired at Etruria, Whieldon-Wedgwood 1756. Length 3″.

15a. Knife, green glaze handle, Barlaston 1940. Length 10″.

16. Beer mug, marbled, thrown and turned, strip handle, Whieldon-Wedgwood 1758. Hgt. 5″.

17. Fragment, sweet meat basket, marbled, crow's foot design, shell shape, Whieldon-Wedgwood 1756. Dia. 3½″.

18. Teapot, marbled, pressed and turned, rolled handle, unglazed, "slurry" finish inside, Whieldon-Wedgwood 1756. Hgt. 4″.

19. Teapot cover, glazed example of the same type as catalogue no. 18, Whieldon-Wedgwood 1756. Hgt. 1″.

20. Cream jug, marbled, pressed and turned, on 3 feet, found at Whieldon factory site, Whieldon-Wedgwood 1756. Hgt. 3½″.

21. Two fragments, bowl, marbled, pressed and turned, found at the Whieldon factory site, Whieldon-Wedgwood 1756. Hgt. 1½″.

22. Fragment, bowl, blue scratch ware, salt glaze, Whieldon-Wedgwood 1755. Hgt. 1½″.

23. Fragment, bowl, marbled, example of the thinnest of potting and the definite

lines marbling achieved during Wedgwood's partnership with Whieldon, found at Whieldon factory site, Whieldon-Wedgwood 1758. Hgt. 1¼″.

24. Fragment, saucer, inlaid marbling, pressed and turned (an example of inlaid ware, later perfected during the Etruria period) Whieldon-Wedgwood 1759. Hgt. 1″.

25. Fragment, trencher, combed slip decoration, Whieldon, 1750. Dia. 3″.

26. Teapot foot mold, shell pattern, found at Whieldon factory site, Whieldon-Wedgwood 1758. Length 3″.

27. Teapot, Egyptian black, forerunner of black basalt, thrown and turned with applied spout, handle and three feet made from mold (catalogue no. 26), found at the Whieldon factory site, Whieldon-Wedgwood 1758. Hgt. 5″.

28. Teapot, Egyptian black, lead glaze, pear shape, found at Whieldon factory site, Whieldon-Wedgwood 1757. Hgt. 4″.

29. Tea caddy, Egyptian black, pear shape, found at Whieldon factory site, over fired specimen showing blistering, Whieldon-Wedgwood 1757. Hgt. 3″.

30. Tea caddy cover, heavy lead glazed example of cover for catalogue no. 29, found at the Whieldon factory site, Whieldon-Wedgwood 1757. Hgt. 1¼″.

31. Cream jug, marbled, earliest example of side handle, pear shape, Whieldon-Wedgwood 1756. Hgt. 2½″.

32. Teapot, red ware, inlaid marbled bands, white slip bands at top of spout and handle, thrown, turned, band applied and serration created while revolving on the lathe, applied spout, turned foot, found at Whieldon factory site, Whieldon-Wedgwood 1756. Hgt. 4″.

33. Teapot, biscuit, tortoiseshell cover, early example of applied ornamentation, crabstock handle and spout, found at Whieldon factory site, Whieldon-Wedgwood 1758. Hgt. 3½″.

34. Pitcher mold, four leaves used for forming decoration as applied on cata-

logue no. 33, found at Whieldon factory site. 1756. Dia. 1½".

35. Teapot cover, tortoiseshell, bird ornament, applied leaf design found at Whieldon factory site, Whieldon-Wedgwood 1758. Hgt. 1".

36. Model, teapot, embossed *Imp and Arabesque* pattern, salt glaze, Burslem 1762. Hgt. 4½".

37. Teapot cover, red ware, *Imp and Arabesque* design, rabbit knob, found at the Whieldon factory site, Whieldon-Wedgwood 1757. Hgt. 1".

BURSLEM PERIOD

38. Model, cornucopia, salt glaze, used to make white wall vase (catalogue no. 39), Burslem 1760. Hgt. 12".

39. Cornucopia, salt glaze, *Flora* with elaborate scalloped floral decoration, Burslem 1760. Hgt. 12".

40. Model for basket, salt glaze, earliest form of basket work, Burslem 1763. Hgt. 5¾".

41. Oval basket, made from catalogue no. 40, salt glaze, Burslem 1763. Hgt. 3½".

42. Model, tea caddy, *Cauliflower,* model from which the Cauliflower ware and green glaze was developed, No. 7 in Josiah Wedgwood's Experiment Book, Burslem 1759. Hgt. 5".

43. Model, tea caddy cover, *Cauliflower,* Burslem 1759. Hgt. 1½".

44. Model, teapot spout, used for *Cabbage* pattern, green glaze, Burslem 1759. Length 6".

45. Model, teapot spout used for *Leaf* pattern, green glaze, Burslem 1759. Length 4½".

46. Teapot, green glaze, *Cabbage* pattern, Burslem 1759. Hgt. 5".

47. Model, cream jug, *Cabbage* pattern, salt glaze, used in making catalogue no. 48, Burslem 1759. Hgt. 3½".

48. Cream jug, green glaze, *Cabbage* pattern, Burslem 1759. Hgt. 2½".

49. Model, teapot spout, Rosso Antico, inscribed "1 dish pot," crabstock, found

at Whieldon factory site, Whieldon-Wedgwood 1756. Hgt. 3".

49a. Dessert plate, green glaze, *Vine and Strawberry* pattern, Burslem 1759. Dia. 8¾".

50. Teapot, *Cauliflower,* Etruria 1760. Hgt. 7".

51. Model, compotier, salt glaze, bird on diaper background, Burslem 1763. Hgt. 11".

52. Model, pear wood, hexagonal shape, used for catalogue no. 53, carved by John Coward, Burslem 1765. Hgt. 11".

53. Vase and cover, early cream ware, hexagonal shape, pressed, head handles, acanthus leaf decoration, Burslem 1765. Hgt. 11".

54. Vase and cover, early cream ware, pressed, flutes and borders, strip handles, Burslem 1768. Hgt. 11".

56. Vase and cover, early Queen's Ware, pear shape, thrown and turned, two handles, applied masks, acorn knob on cover, Burslem 1768. Hgt. 10½".

57. Fragment, plate, stone ware, salt glaze, gadroon edge, one of Wedgwood's earliest dinnerware shapes, Burslem 1763. Dia. 4".

58. Fragment, plate, stone ware, salt glaze, early dinnerware shapes, Burslem 1763. Dia. 2½".

ETRURIA PERIOD
BLACK BASALT

59a. Vase and cover, encaustic painting, one of the first day's throwing at Etruria, June 13, 1769, at the opening of Etruria. Six of these vases were thrown by Josiah Wedgwood while Thomas Bentley turned the wheel. Hgt. 10".

60. Teapot and cover, black basalt, encaustic painting, widow knob, presented by Josiah Wedgwood to George Barnett's wife upon the birth of twins after reprimanding her husband for being late for work, Etruria 1788. Hgt. 5".

60a. Vase, black basalt, encaustic decoration, Etruscan style, Etruria 1780. Hgt. 11".

62a. Vase, black basalt, encaustic decoration, Etruscan style, thrown and turned, Etruria 1784. Hgt. 11".

63. Spill vase for tapers, black basalt, encaustic decoration, thrown and turned, white inlaid border, Etruria 1778. Hgt. 3½".

64. Spill vase for tapers, black basalt, encaustic painting, Etruscan style, Etruria 1778. Hgt. 4".

65. Cup and saucer, black basalt, encaustic painted border, Etruria 1778. Hgt. 2½".

66. Ink stand, black basalt, encaustic border design, glazed inside, Etruria 1778. Hgt. 3½".

67. Pen tray, black basalt, unusual script mark, Wedgwood & Bentley, molded Sphinx, Etruria 1769. Hgt. 3".

68. Vase and cover, black basalt, two handles with rams head masks, Etruria 1772. Hgt. 4".

69. Ink stand, black basalt, ink well and sand box in basket, bow handle, pressed, Etruria 1784. Hgt. 3½".

70. Vase, black basalt, thrown and turned, pressed handle, with cupid head masks, Etruria 1782. Hgt. 8".

71. Vase, black basalt, thrown and turned, mask handles, Etruria 1782. Hgt. 9¼".

72. Ink stand, black basalt, eagle head ends, pressed, Etruria 1786. Hgt. 6".

73. Pipe Head, black basalt, Etruria 1782. Hgt. 2".

74. Vase, black basalt, three handles, thrown and turned, fluted foot, Etruria 1786. Hgt. 7".

75. Lamp, black basalt, Roman shape, Etruria 1784. Hgt. 2".

76. Stirrup cup, black basalt, hares head, glazed interior, Etruria 1782. Hgt. 4".

77. Teapot, black basalt, widow knob, thrown and turned, Etruria 1778. Hgt. 6".

78. Coffee pot and cover, black basalt, engine turned, fluted, widow knob, Etruria 1788. Hgt. 9½".

79. Lamp, black basalt, molded, fluted decoration, first indication of *Wellesley*

embossment, Etruria 1782. Hgt. 6½".

80. Vase, reversible cover becomes candlestick, black basalt, thrown and turned, engine lathe turning, fluting, and applied handles, Etruria 1773. Hgt. 7".

81. Ewer, black basalt, engine turned, fluted decoration, *Boys at Play,* Etruria 1775. Hgt. 11½".

82. Vase and cover, black basalt, engine turned, satyr handles and acorn knob, Etruria 1778. Hgt. 11½".

83. Tripod vase, black basalt, engine turned, leopard supports, three widow figures for knob, Etruria 1790. Hgt. 11½".

84. Vase and cover, black basalt, molded with flutes and drapery festoons, two scrolled handles, Etruria 1778. Hgt. 10½".

85. Candlestick, black basalt, pedestal with branch, engine lathe turning, fluted ornaments, Etruria 1790. Hgt. 9½".

86. Vase, black basalt, thrown and turned, fish tail handle, key runner border, drapery festoons, two masks, Etruria 1775. Hgt. 10½".

87. Vase and cover, black basalt, molded decorations, mask rams head handles, Etruria 1778. Hgt. 5".

88. Vase, black basalt, Arabesque scroll, honeysuckle and grape embossed decorations, early example of *Patrician* pattern, Etruria 1775. Hgt. 6¾".

89. Vase, black basalt, engine turned, drapery festoons, applied acanthus leaves, masked handles, Etruria 1778. Hgt. 7".

89a. Vase, black basalt, applied mask and drapery festoons, Etruria 1775. Hgt. 15".

90. Vase, black basalt, engine turned, applied *Boys with Wreath* and laurel border, Etruria 1784. Hgt. 7½".

91. Vase, black basalt, engine turned, flutes, applied festoon, and scroll handles, husk design, Etruria 1772. Hgt. 9½".

92. Vase, black basalt, engine turned, applied ornaments, Etruria 1775. Hgt. 10¼".

93. Bust, *John Locke,* black basalt, Etruria 1778. Hgt. 9½".

94. Bust, *Sir Isaac Newton,* black basalt, Etruria 1782. Hgt. 9".

94a. Bust, *Josiah Wedgwood,* black basalt, modeled by E. A. Austin from monument in Stoke-on-Trent Church — to commemorate the Bicentenary of Josiah Wedgwood's birth, Etruria 1930. Hgt. 18".

95. Medallion, *Charles I,* black basalt, kings and queens of England series, Etruria 1772. Dia. 2".

96. Medallion, *Edward 1,* black basalt, kings and queens of England series, Etruria 1772. Dia. 2".

97. Medallion, *Mary Queen of Scots,* black basalt, kings and queens of England series, Etruria 1772. Dia. 2".

98. Medallion, *Edward VI,* black basalt, kings and queens of England series, Etruria 1772. Dia. 2".

99. Medallion, *Jean Jacques Rousseau,* black basalt, Etruria 1773. Dia. 1¾".

100. Shank seal, black basalt, intaglio, *Charles James Fox,* Etruria 1782. Dia. 1".

100a. Historic Medals, black basalt and biscuit models, modeled on both sides, Etruria 1776. Dia. 1¼".

   1. Hannibal at the Gates of Rome, and Spain Succored.
   2. Caesar Crossing the Rubicon, and Flight of the Senate.
   3. Alliance of Romans with Hiers, and Aid of a Faithful Ally.
   4. Head of Marius, and Defeat of Cimbri.
   5. Model for No. 1.
   6. Valour of Horatius Coceles, and Constancy of Scabola.
   7. Anthony and Cleopatra, and Battle of Actium.
   8. Oath of Brutus, and Rome Free from under the Controls.
   9. Head of Regulus, and Virtue of Regulus.
   10. Augustus, and Reign of Augustus.
   11. Head of Cato, and Death of Cato.
   12. Battle of Pharsalia, and Humanity of Caesar.

101. Plaque, *Zeno,* black basalt, figure mounted on Rosso Antico, black basalt frame, Etruria 1785. Dia. 14¾".

102. Plaque, *Herculean figure,* black basalt, slightly bronzed, Etruria 1781. Dia. 15".

103. Bust, *Homer,* black basalt, Etruria 1778. Hgt. 13".

104. Vase, black basalt, replica of 18th century vase made to stand in niche in Winnington Hall, Cheshire, for Lord Mond, fluted lattice decoration with acanthus leaves, scrolled handles, pear shape, Etruria 1922. Hgt. 4 ft.

105. Vase, black basalt, replica of 18th century vase made to stand in niche in Winnington Hall, Cheshire for Lord Mond, pear shape, Etruria 1922. Hgt. 4 ft.

107. Bust, *Pindar,* black basalt, Etruria 1777. Hgt. 19½".

107a. Bust, *Mercury,* black basalt, modeled by Hoskins and Grant, in 1779, Etruria 1907. Hgt. 18".

108. Plaque, *Peter the Great,* black basalt, Etruria 1777. Dia. 18".

109. Chimney plaque, *Death of a Roman Warrior,* black basalt, Etruria 1782. Length 25".

JASPER

110. Jasper Cameo ring which belonged to Josiah Wedgwood, white on blue, Etruria 1785.

111. Drawing, *Chessmen* by John Flaxman, 1784 from which jasper chessmen were produced. Length 18", Hgt. 6".

112. Wax model, chess king, modeled by Flaxman from the original drawing (catalogue no. 111), Etruria 1784. Hgt. 3½".

113. Biscuit model, chess king, marked trial, partly glazed, modeled by Flaxman, Etruria 1784. Hgt. 4½".

114. Chess king, jasper, modeled by Flaxman, Etruria 1790. Hgt. 3½".

115. Chess king, jasper on blue jasper dip

base, from Flaxman's original model, Etruria 1865. Hgt. 3½".

116. Chess king, black basalt, shape no. 4513, modeled by Arnold Machin, Etruria 1939. Hgt. 5".

117. Chess king, terra cotta, shape no. 4513, modeled by Arnold Machin, Etruria 1939. Hgt. 4¾".

118. Chess king, Queen's Ware, shape no. 4513, modeled by Arnold Machin, Etruria 1939. Hgt. 5½".

119. Chess set, jasper, modeled by John Flaxman, Etruria 1790.

120. Chess king, Queen's Ware, shape no. 4513, modeled by Arnold Machin, cream color and lavender, Etruria 1939.

121. Chess queen, jasper, white figure on lilac jasper dip base, modeled by John Flaxman, in 1784, Etruria 1865. Hgt. 4".

122. Chess Jester, Queen's Ware figure on inlaid base, cream color, black inlay on cream base, from Flaxman's original model, Etruria 1880. Hgt. 3".

123. Chess Jester, Queen's Ware, on inlaid base, cream color, cream inlay on black base made from Flaxman's original model. Etruria 1880. Hgt. 3".

124. Four chessmen, bishop and three pawns, black basalt, designed by Arnold Machin, shape no. 4513, Etruria 1939.

125. Model, medallion *Diomedes,* first of a series showing the production processes in the making of a medallion, Etruria 1777. Width 3".

126. Wax Model, *Diomedes,* medallion production series, Etruria 1777. Width 3".

127. Trial, medallion, *Diomedes,* showing blistering, in Josiah Wedgwood's development of jasper for medallions, Etruria 1777. Dia. 4".

128. Medallion, *Diomedes,* jasper, perfected piece, Etruria 1777. Dia. 3".

129. Medallion, *Sidney Cove, Hope Attended by Peace,* and *Art and Labor,* jasper, made from clay brought from Australia by Sir Joseph Banks, Etruria 1789. Dia. 2½".

130. Medallion, *Sidney Cove, Hope Attended by Peace,* and *Art and Labor,* Queen's Ware, cream color on lavender, present production of Sidney Cove medallion, Barlaston 1947. Dia. 2¾".

131. Medallion, *Shakespeare,* jasper, white on blue, Etruria 1780. Dia. 2".

132. Medallion, *Head of Emperor Augustus,* jasper, white on blue, Etruria 1780. Dia. 3¾".

133. Medallion, *River Goddess,* jasper, white on blue, Etruria 1780. Dia. 3½".

134. Medallion, *River God,* jasper, white on blue, Etruria 1780. Dia. 3½".

135. Medallion, *Mother and Child,* jasper, white on sage green, Etruria 1780. Dia. 3⅞".

136. Medallion, *Venus and Cupids,* jasper, white on blue, Etruria 1780. Dia. 4⅝".

137. Medallion, *Domestic Subject,* jasper, white on green, designed by Lady Templetown, Etruria 1780. Dia. 4⅝".

138. Medallion, *Prince William,* jasper, white on blue, Etruria 1780. Dia. 3⅛".

139. Medallion, *Jonas Hanway,* jasper, white, Etruria 1780. Dia. 4½".

140. Medallion, *Two Muses,* medallion of Gessner, jasper, white on blue, Etruria 1780. Dia. 3¼".

141. Medallion, *Sportive Love,* jasper, white on blue, designed by Lady Templetown, Etruria 1780. Dia. 4¾".

142. Medallion, *Marriage of Cupid and Psyche,* jasper, white on blue, modeled by William Hackwood from the Marlborough Gem, Etruria 1776. Dia. 3".

143. Medallion, *George III,* jasper, white on blue, gilt frame, Etruria 1780. Hgt. 3¼".

144. Medallion, *Sir Joshua Reynolds,* jasper, white on blue, Etruria 1780. Dia. 4".

145. Medallion, *Queen Charlotte,* jasper, white on blue, gilt frame, Etruria 1780. Hgt. 3¾".

146. Portrait Medallion, *John Philip Kemble,* jasper, white on green, Etruria 1782. Hgt. 7".

147. Model, medallion, *Benjamin Franklin,*

biscuit, Etruria 1778. Dia. 4½".

148. Model, medallion, *Benjamin Franklin*, terra cotta, modeled by Nini, Etruria 1777. Dia. 4½".

149. Medallion, *Benjamin Franklin*, jasper, Etruria 1780. Dia. 4".

150. Medallion, *Benjamin Franklin*, jasper, made for the opening of Franklin's house in London, June 1947. This medallion represents the first jasper made at Barlaston. Dia. 4".

151. Model, *Lafayette*, biscuit, Etruria 1777. Dia. 3".

152. Medallion, *Lafayette*, jasper, white on blue, made for the opening of Franklin's house in London, Barlaston, June 1947. Dia. 3".

154. Medallion, *Venus and Cupid*, jasper, white on blue, gilt, Etruria 1786. Hgt. 8".

155. Portrait Medallion, *Honora Edgeworth*, jasper, white, trial piece marked "one of 1559, one of 3614, no cobalt in it, last mixture," Etruria 1786. Dia. 2½".

156. Portrait Medallion, *Honora Edgeworth*, jasper, white on black, trial marked, "ground and head of 3615 black jasper wash," Etruria 1786. Dia. 2½".

157. Wax model, portrait medallion, notable lady of the period, red on black, Etruria 1780. Dia. 4½".

158. Wax model, medallion, *Sarah Wedgwood*, wife of Josiah Wedgwood modeled by Joachim Smith, Etruria 1774. Width 5½".

159. Medallion, *Alexander the Great*, jasper, white on blue, Etruria 1776. Hgt. 3½".

159a. Medallion, *Oliver Wendell Holmes*, jasper, white on blue, black edge, Etruria 1930. Dia. 6".

160. Vase, *Apotheosis of Homer*, jasper, white on blue, Etruria 1785. Hgt. 18".

161. Vase, *Judgment of Paris*, jasper, white on blue, modeled by John Flaxman 1780. Hgt. 19".

162, 163. Two plaques, *Dancing Hours*, jasper, white on blue, modeled by John Flaxman 1775. Length 1' 2" each.

164. Replica of vase used on top of Princess Elizabeth's Wedding cake. *Dancing Hours*, white on blue, November 20, 1947, Barlaston 1947. Hgt. 6½".

165. Replica of six miniature vases used on Princess Elizabeth's Wedding cake, November 20, 1947, *Dancing Hours*, modeled by John Flaxman 1775, Barlaston 1947. Hgt. 4".

166. Two Hair Brushes, cameos, jasper, white on blue, set in sterling silver mounts 1890, *Cupids* and *Sportive Love*, designed by Lady Templetown, Etruria 1779. Length 5".

166a. Perfume Bottle, jasper, white on blue, Etruria 1790. Hgt. 4½".

167. Trophy Plate, *Psyche Being Bound to a Tree by Cupid*, the trophies are applied in the swags of the border, jasper, white on blue, Etruria 1880. Dia. 8".

168. Plaque, *Choice of Hercules*, jasper, white on blue, modeled by William Hackwood, 1777, Etruria 1783. Dia. 9½".

169. Plaque, *Bacchus and Panther*, modeled by William Hackwood, jasper, white, Etruria 1775. Hgt. 5".

170. Wax model and biscuit model, rural subject, designed by Lady Templetown, modeled by William Hackwood, one of a group of rural scenes, Etruria 1783. Hgt. 4½".

171. Plaque, *George Washington*, jasper, white on blue, Etruria 1920. Hgt. 8".

172. Biscuit model, *Sportive Love*, jasper, designed by Lady Templetown, modeled by William Hackwood, Etruria 1783. Hgt. 3".

173. Ink stand, imitation of Roman ruin, jasper, white on blue, acanthus leaf decoration, Etruria 1786. Hgt. 4".

174. Tea cup, *Poor Maria*, jasper, white on blue, designed by Lady Templetown, Etruria 1785. Hgt. 2".

175. Cup and saucer, jasper, white on green, acanthus leaf decoration, thrown and turned, cup lapidary polished interior, Etruria 1790. Hgt. 2½".

175a. Cream jug, *Boys at Play*, jasper, white on blue, Etruria 1786. Hgt. 2".

175b. Tea or punch kettle, *Boys at Play*, jasper, white on blue, designed by Lady Templetown, Etruria 1788. Hgt. 5½".

175c. Candlestick, *Ceres*, jasper, white on blue, Etruria 1790. Hgt. 10".

175d. Candlestick, *Pomona*, jasper, white on blue, Etruria 1790. Hgt. 10".

175e. Plaque, *Birth of Bacchus*, jasper, white on blue, modeled by John Flaxman 1782, Etruria 1790. Hgt. 6".

175f. Name cards and biscuit model, *Josiah Wedgwood, F.R.S.*, jasper, blue on white, Etruria 1785. Dia. 2".

175g. Medallion, *Slave in Chains*, "Am I not a man and a brother." Jasper, black on white, modeled by William Hackwood for distribution in the campaign for the abolition of slavery and adopted as the seal of the Slave Emancipation Society of which Wedgwood and Bentley were keen supporters, Etruria 1786. Dia. 1 1/5".

176. Biscuit model for canoe basket (catalogue no. 177), Etruria 1782. Hgt. 5".

177. Canoe basket, three color jasper dip, molded, dipped, engine turned, applied cross pieces and decoration at base, white, blue and yellow, Etruria 1782. Hgt. 5½".

178. Jug, three color jasper dip, diced pattern, thrown and turned, dipped, engine turned, applied crosses and borders, white, blue, and green, Etruria 1784. Hgt. 4½".

179. Vase, three color jasper dip, thrown and turned, dipped, engine turned, applied strap work and acanthus leaves, white, lilac and green, Etruria 1786. Hgt. 5".

180. Tobacco jar, three color jasper dip, thrown and turned, dipped, engine turned, applied laurel and stars, white, black and yellow, Etruria 1880. Hgt. 7½".

181. Custard cup, tear drop shape, jasper dip, applied net work, white on lilac, Etruria 1786. Hgt. 1½".

182. Flower pot, three color jasper dip, white jasper, blue dip, applied green strap work, Etruria 1788. Hgt. 4".

182a. Flower pot, two color dip, white jasper dipped in blue jasper dip, engine turned diced pattern, applied crosses, Etruria 1788. Hgt. 4½".

182b. Vase, four color jasper dip, white, blue, lilac and chocolate, Etruria 1786. Hgt. 7".

183. Plaque, three color cameo production series, no. 1 white jasper background cut to shape, no. 2 same dipped in green jasper dip, no. 3 placed on mold for outline decoration and blue jasper center applied, no. 4 ornaments made in molds and removed ready for application, no. 5 finished cameo. Etruria 1770. Hgt. 5½".

184. Mascara box, ivory, cameo, jasper, blue, white, lilac, *Antinous* mounted in cover, set in gold, mirror inside, ivory compartments for mascara and rouge with brushes, Etruria 1788. Length 3".

184a. Patch box, ivory, cameo, jasper, white on blue, *Cupids at Play*, mounted in cover, lined with crimson velvet, mirror inside, Etruria 1788. Length 4".

185. Chatelaine, cut steel with three double cameos, white on blue, *Aurora*, modeled by William Hackwood 1773, and bead, seal of *Jacques Necker*, Etruria 1790. Length 10".

186. Chatelaine, cut steel, seal, watch key and double cameo, jasper, white on blue, *Priam Begging the Body of Hector*, modeled by John Flaxman, Etruria 1790. Length 10".

187. Four jasper beads, applied decoration, used for earrings, rings, beads and other ornaments, Etruria 1786. Dia. ½".

188. Intaglio shank seal, black basalt, *Queen Charlotte*, modeled by William Hackwood, Etruria 1775. Length 1".

189. Cameo, belt buckle, jasper, white on blue, *Polymnia*, modeled by John Flaxman, steel mount by Matthew Boulton, Etruria 1790. Hgt. 3½".

190. Cameo, belt buckle, jasper, white on blue, *Domestic Employment*, designed by Lady Templetown, modeled by William Hackwood, steel mount by Matthew Boulton, Etruria 1790. Hgt. 3½".

191. Frame of 43 cameos, steel mounted brooch and earrings in center, Etruria 1790. Hgt. 14".

192. Frame of 26 cameos, bracelet in center with split silver mounting, Etruria 1790. Hgt. 16".

193. Frame of 15 cameos, buckles and buttons, jasper, white on blue, with steel mounts by Matthew Boulton, Etruria 1790. Hgt. 15".

194. Frame of cameos with *Sidney Cove* medallion in center, Etruria 1770-1790.

195. Frame of trials for jasper, cameos and intaglios, Etruria 1770 to 1780. Hgt. 16".

196. Sarcophagus with two vases, jasper, white on blue, *Marriage of Cupid and Psyche*, modeled by William Hackwood 1776, Etruria 1788, vases on top were broken and replaced at a later date. Hgt. 8½".

196a. Bulb Pot, jasper, white on green, *Venus and Cupid, Terpsichore*, modeled by John Flaxman 1775, Etruria 1778. Hgt. 7½".

197. Vase, jasper, white on blue, *Cupids*, honeysuckle and acanthus leaves, scroll handles, Etruria 1782. Hgt. 7".

198. Candelabrum, *Winter*, jasper, white on blue, modeled by William Hackwood 1777, Etruria 1780. Hgt. 10".

199. Candelabrum, *Summer*, jasper, white on blue, modeled by William Hackwood 1777, Etruria 1780. Hgt. 10".

200. Presentation vase, jasper, black and white fluting, designed by Victor Skellern to commemorate a visit paid by Queen Mary to Etruria and Barlaston, July 27, 1939.

200a. Presentation vase, jasper, white on black, *Dancing Hours*, designed to commemorate a visit by Queen Mary, April 23, 1913 to Etruria.

201. Drum, white jasper, blue ends, *Sacrifice Figures*, designed by John Flaxman 1779, Etruria 1786. Hgt. 4½".

204. Urn, jasper, white on green, *Melpomene and Erato*, modeled by John Flaxman 1777, Etruria 1930. Hgt. 12".

205. Apollo vase, jasper dip, white on blue, designed by John E. Goodwin for the bicentenary of Josiah Wedgwood's birth, 1730-1930, Etruria 1930. Hgt. 9½". Latin inscription: "CC Postnatum Conditorem Anno Viget Ars Etruriae Redintegrata." Figure of *Apollo* on cover.

206. Flower pot, bas-relief, white on blue, *Sacrifice Figures*, jasper figures applied to stoneware body, introduced 1880, made from 18th century molds, Etruria 1939. Hgt. 4".

207. Jug, bas-relief, white on green, Etruscan shape, jasper figures made from 18th century Wedgwood molds applied to stoneware body, introduced 1880, Etruria 1939. Hgt. 6".

207a. Jug, bas-relief, white on crimson, jasper figures made from 18th century Wedgwood molds applied to stoneware body, introduced 1880, Etruria 1939. Hgt. 6".

208. Tobacco jar, jasper dip, green on white, thrown and turned, applied white ornaments, Etruria 1790. Hgt. 6½".

209. Biscuit model for lyre vase, catalogue no. 210, Etruria 1782. Hgt. 6½".

210. Vase, lyre shape, jasper dip, blue on white, applied white decoration, Etruria 1782. Hgt. 6½".

210a. Vase, solid white jasper, *Maternal Affection*, designed by Lady Templetown, modeled by William Hackwood, Etruria 1783. Hgt. 12".

211. Cup and saucer, jasper, white on blue, *Maternal Subjects*, designed by Lady Templetown, modeled by William Hackwood, Etruria 1783. Hgt. 3".

211a. Vase and cover, jasper, white on green,
& *Sacrifice of Hymen* and *Marriage of*
211b. *Cupid and Psyche,* modeled by William

Hackwood 1774 and 1776, Etruria 1776. Hgt. 8¼".

212a. Tea Kettle, jasper, white on blue, *Infant Academy*, designed by Sir Joshua Reynolds, Etruria 1778. Hgt. 6".

213. Bowl, jasper, white on blue, *Domestic Employment*, designed by Lady Templetown modeled by William Hackwood, Etruria 1783. Hgt. 4".

214. Teapot, jasper, white on blue, *Domestic Employment*, designed by Lady Templetown modeled by William Hackwood, Etruria 1788. Hgt. 5½".

215. Tray, jasper, white on blue, Etruria 1788. Dia. 13¼".

216. Custard cup and stand, jasper, white on blue, Etruria 1784. Hgt. 2½".

217. Bowl, jasper, white on lilac, *Domestic Employment* and *Boys at Play*, designed by Lady Templetown, modeled by William Hackwood, Etruria 1784. Hgt. 3".

218. Cup, jasper, white on green, *Whimsical Figure*, designed by Lady Templetown, modeled by William Hackwood, Etruria 1783. Hgt. 3".

219. Coffee can and saucer, jasper, white on green, Etruria 1788. Hgt. 4".

220. Teapot, jasper, white on green, *Flora*, modeled by John Flaxman, silver shape, Etruria 1790. Hgt. 5½".

221. Teapot, jasper, white on green, acanthus leaves and bell flower, Etruria 1789. Hgt. 6½".

222. Punch ladle, jasper, blue and white, twisted handle, mask head, grapevine border, Etruria 1785. Length 19".

223. Biscuit model, for teapot catalogue no. 220, Etruria 1790. Hgt. 4½".

224. Teapot, jasper, chocolate on drab, *Flora*, modeled by John Flaxman, Etruria 1789. Hgt. 5⅛".

225. Paint box, jasper, white on blue, *The Boar Hunt*, *Bringing Home the Game* and *Music*, modeled by William Hackwood, made for ladies to use in painting china, 15 pieces, palette, paint cups, holder, box and cover, Etruria 1782. Hgt. 2½".

226. Custard set, four covered cups and tray, jasper, white on blue, Etruria 1784. Width 6½".

227. Pipe, jasper dip, white and blue, thrown and turned, applied stem with runner bands, Etruria 1784. Length 3".

QUEEN'S WARE

229. Queen's Ware, Josiah Wedgwood's catalogue of 1770, showing covered dishes, lattice bowl, basket weave plate, orange bowl, nut dish, etc.

230. Covered orange bowl, Queen's Ware, pierced, Etruria 1769. Hgt. 9".

231. Biscuit model, pierced basket, for catalogue no. 232, Etruria 1780. Hgt. 5".

232. Basket, Queen's Ware, pierced, made from catalogue no. 231, Etruria 1780. Hgt. 5".

233. Nut Basket, Queen's Ware, pierced, Etruria 1780. Hgt. 3".

234. Biscuit model, jug, Etruria 1790. Hgt. 4½".

235. Covered soup tureen, Queen's Ware, *Bewick Scenes*, printed in black by Sadler and Green, Etruria 1769. Hgt. 11".

238. Plate no. 81, part of the original service made for Catherine the Great of Russia, Queen's Ware, *Ruin*, sepia with green frog crest, Etruria 1774. Dia. 10".

239. Plate, *Russian Service* design, Queen's Ware, multicolor, *Aysgarth Bridge, Yorkshire*, Etruria 1774. Dia. 9".

240. Plate, *Russian Service* design, Queen's Ware, multicolor, *Welbeck, Nottinghamshire*, Etruria 1774. Dia. 9".

241. Plate, *Russian Service* design, Queen's Ware, multicolor, *Coverham Abbey, Coverdale, Yorkshire*, Etruria 1774. Dia. 9".

242. Plate, Queen's Ware, painted border no. 266, *Wheat* design, blue and brown, from early pattern book, Etruria 1777. Dia. 8".

243. Compotier, Queen's Ware, painted border no. 266, *Wheat* design, blue and brown, from early pattern book, Etruria 1777. Dia. 8".

244. Covered dish, painted Ivy border, green, crest of *Brickdale* family Somerset and Gloucestershire, England, Queen's Ware, Etruria 1780. Length 9".

245. Fern pot and stand, Queen's Ware, painted red and black border, Etruria 1774. Hgt. 4½".

246. Jug, Queen's Ware, painted grape festoon and morning glories, green, blue and purple, Etruria 1778. Hgt. 9".

247. Sauce tureen and cover, Queen's Ware, brown lines, traced knob and handles, Etruria 1773. Hgt. 6".

248. Custard cup, Queen's Ware, engine turned, Etruria 1780. Hgt. 3½".

249. Section from supper tray, Queen's Ware, painted border, green, red and brown, Etruria 1776. Length 11".

250. Section from supper tray, Queen's Ware, painted border, green, blue and brown, Etruria 1776. Length 11".

251. Herring Dish, Queen's Ware, center design of embossed fish, Etruria 1769. Length 11".

252. Jug, Queen's Ware, painted red and brown border, monogram "J.F.", Blivick scene, Etruria 1775. Hgt. 4½".

253. Cream jug, Queen's Ware, painted *Strawberry Leaf* pattern, green, brown and gold, from early pattern book, Etruria 1775. Hgt. 3½".

254. Bowl, Queen's Ware, *Antique* border, yellow and black, Etruria 1775. Hgt. 3½".

255. Compotier, Queen's Ware, painted border, green, blue, and brown, Etruria 1775. Length 12½".

256. Section of supper tray, Queen's Ware, *Antique* border, yellow and black, Etruria 1775. Length 13¾".

257. Cream dish, on plinth, Queen's Ware, painted *Lag and Feather* border, blue and brown, Etruria 1775. Hgt. 4⅞".

258. Plate, Queen's Ware, painted *Lag and Feather* border, blue and brown, Etruria 1775. Dia. 7".

259. Coffee can, fixed stand, Queen's Ware, painted *Honeysuckle* border in red and black, Etruria 1775. Hgt. 3".

260. Covered supper dish, Queen's Ware, painted *Running Leaf* pattern, green, brown and blue, Etruria 1775. Length 14".

261. Oval dish, Queen's Ware, painted *Vine* border in purple and green, Etruria 1775. Length 17½".

262. Salesmen's catalogue, illustrations by John Taylor Wedgwood, Etruria 1810. Length 8".

263. Jelly mold, Queen's Ware, *Wheat* design in pink and brown, Etruria 1786. Hgt. 6½".

263a. Paint box, Queen's Ware, for ladies use in painting china, molded and pressed, dipped in black slip, scraped, revealing white flutes, Dolphin finial, Etruria 1792. Hgt. 4".

264. Two custard cups, Queen's Ware, painted
& *Watteau* subjects in multicolor,
265. Etruria 1782. Hgt. 1½".
266. Pickle dish, Queen's Ware, leaf shape, Etruria 1774. Dia. 4".

267. Pair of candlesticks, Queen's Ware,
& painted *Watteau* subjects, multicolor,
267a. Etruria 1782. Hgt. 7½".

268. Jug, Queen's Ware, painted border and spray, multicolor, marked "made for J. Boulton," Etruria 1778. Hgt. 5¾".

269. Jug, Queen's Ware, made for Staffordshire Volunteer regiment, Etruria 1786. Hgt. 8".

271. Sauce tureen and cover with fixed stand, Queen's Ware, green and brown, Etruria 1786. Hgt. 5½".

272. Center for jelly mold, Queen's Ware, multicolor, painted in the Chelsea studios, Etruria 1774. Hgt. 9".

273. Soup plate, Queen's Ware, painted *Vine and Grape* border, purple and green, Etruria 1790. Dia. 10".

274. Original Shape Book of Josiah Wedgwood, Etruria 1770.

275. Oval dish, Queen's Ware, *Shell Edge* shape 9 in original shape book, gadroon edge in blue and gold, crest in center, marked "Foy Lisbon" in colors

276. Plate, Queen's Ware, *Shell Edge* shape 9 in original shape book, *Mared* pattern in blue, Etruria 1770. Dia. 10".

278. Plate, Queen's Ware, *Concave* shape 8 in original shape book, painted red and black border, Etruria 1790. Dia. 10".

279. Plate, Queen's Ware, *Concave* shape 8 in original shape book, border painted at Etruria, center decoration painted in France, for French market, Etruria 1782. Dia. 10".

280. Plate, Queen's Ware, *New Feather Edge* shape 2 in original shape book, green and purple trial painting, Etruria 1772. Dia. 10".

281. Plate, Queen's Ware, *Royal* shape 4 in original shape book, *Antique* border in purple, Etruria 1778. Dia. 10".

282. Plate, Queen's Ware, *Old Feather Edge* shape 1 in original shape book, Liverpool Birds design printed in black by Sadler and Green, Etruria 1770. Dia. 8".

282a. Plate, *Queen's* shape 3 in original shape book, Bewick pattern printed by Sadler and Green, Etruria 1778. Dia. 10".

283. Bread and butter plate, Queen's Ware, *New Feather Edge* Shell Shape 2 in original shape book, Etruria 1773. Dia. 6".

284. Saucer, Queen's Ware, *Shell Edge* Shape 9 in original shape book, traces of leaf gold, Etruria 1770. Dia. 5".

285. Glacier, Queen's Ware, thrown and turned, hand pierced and relief decorations, Etruria 1773. Hgt. 10".

286. Glacier, Queen's Ware, thrown and turned, Etruria 1773. Hgt. 15".

287. Compotier, Queen's Ware, *Vine* border in brown, Etruria 1778. Length 8½".

288. Sandwich Set, Queen's Ware, four section tray, stand in center for two mustard and relish pots, brown and yellow border, Etruria 1776. Hgt. 5".

289. Basket and cover, Queen's Ware, molded husk and flute design, bow handle, Etruria 1785. Hgt. 5".

290. Cruet, Queen's Ware, oil and vinegar bottles in basket, key runner border, Etruria 1782. Hgt. 5".

291. Supper tray, Queen's Ware, four sections with bowl in center on mahogany tray, brown lines, Etruria 1780. Length 24".

292. Plate, Queen's Ware, *Queen's Shape,* printed in black by Sadler and Green, Etruria 1772. Dia. 10".

293. Plate, *Concave* Shape, dotted border and crest in red, Etruria 1790. Dia. 10".

294. Plate, Queen's Ware, *Concave* Shape, line border, crest of *Lord Anson* in brown, Etruria 1784. Dia. 10".

295. Plate, Queen's Ware, *Queen's* Shape, printed in black by Sadler and Green, Etruria 1772. Dia. 10".

296. Plates, Queen's Ware, *Concave* Shape,
& border painted at Etruria, center de-
297. sign painted in France for French market, Etruria 1782. Dia. 10".

299. Cup and Saucer, Queen's Ware, Shell Edge Shape, *Liverpool Birds,* printed in black by Sadler and Green, Etruria 1772. Hgt. 2".

300. Six plates, Queen's Ware, *Agricultural Implement Series,* designs in yellow, Etruria 1780. Dia. 5".

301. Sauce tureen and cover, Queen's Ware, dotted border and crest in red and black, Etruria 1790. Hgt. 5".

302. Mug, Queen's Ware, *Hunting Scene* printed in black by Sadler and Green, Etruria 1772. Hgt. 6".

303. Tea caddy, Queen's Ware, *Tea Party* design printed in black by Sadler and Green, Etruria 1772. Hgt. 4".

304. Sugar and cover, Queen's Ware, painted *Laurel* border in brown, Etruria 1780. Hgt. 3".

305. Custard cup and cover, Queen's Ware, engine turned, Etruria 1780. Hgt. 4".

306. Covered egg cup, Queen's Ware, engine turned, square plinth, Etruria 1773. Hgt. 4½".

307. Coffee pot, Queen's Ware, Shell Edge Shape, *Liverpool Birds* design, printed

in red by Sadler and Green, Etruria 1772. Hgt. 8".

314. Soup tureen, stand and cover, Queen's Ware, blue, red and brown, Etruria 1780. Hgt. 11".

325. Custard cup, Queen's Ware, painted *Oak* border, green and brown, Etruria 1775. Hgt. 3½".

PORTLAND VASE

329. Admission Card to the first viewing of Josiah Wedgwood's original copy of the Portland Vase placed on exhibit at Greek Street, Soho, 1790.

330. Plaster model of Portland Vase. It was from this model that the final Portland Vase was modeled, Etruria 1786. Hgt. 10".

331. Model of sarcophagus for Portland Vase, signed by William Hackwood, May 18th, 1791, Etruria. Width 4".

332. First trial for ornamentation on base of Portland Vase, white on black jasper, Etruria 1786. Dia. 4".

333. Model for sarcophagus of Portland Vase, signed by William Hackwood, August 15th 1791, Etruria. Width 4".

334. Model for sarcophagus of Portland Vase "*Sacrifice of Iphigenia*" signed by William Hackwood, December 30th, 1791, Etruria. Length 9".

335. Biscuit models of figures on Portland Vase, Etruria 1786. Length 11".

336. Trial of Portland Vase showing perfection of body, ornaments not adhering to body, Etruria 1787. Hgt. 11".

337. Engraved copper plate from which invitations to view the original copy of the Portland Vase were printed, Etruria 1790. Length 3".

338. Biscuit model for base of Portland Vase, Etruria 1786. Dia. 5".

339. Trial for Portland Vase showing blistering of body, one of the first trials, Etruria 1787. Hgt. 11".

341. Portland Vase No. 25 of the first series made by Josiah Wedgwood. This copy was made in 1793. Josiah completed his first copy in 1790, jasper, white on black. Hgt. 11".

DRY BODIES

342. Flower pot, rosso antico, black ornamentation, Etruria 1783. Hgt. 7".

343. Cup, rosso antico, black basalt, Egyptian ornaments, glazed interior, Etruria 1785. Hgt. 2½".

344. Bulb pot, cane, imitation of bamboo, glazed interior, Etruria 1785. Hgt. 5".

345. Lamp, rosso antico, black basalt ornament on Roman shape, Etruria 1786. Hgt. 2".

346. Bough pot, cane, painted red, green and blue decoration, engine turned, Etruria 1790. Hgt. 9".

347. Vase, cane, engine turned, applied drab decorations, *Vine* pattern, Etruria 1795. Hgt. 6".

348. Bulb pot, rosso antico, semi-circular shape, embossed *Cupid and Wreath* decoration, Etruria 1783. Hgt. 6".

349. Vase, cane, engine turned with applied *Ivy* design in rosso antico, Etruria 1798. Hgt. 7".

350. Bulb pot, oval, engine turned basket design, Etruria 1797. Hgt. 4½".

351. Bough pot, cane, semi-circular, embossed basket design, Etruria 1797. Hgt. 4½".

352. Flower holder, cane, imitation of bamboo, glazed interior, Etruria 1788. Hgt. 11".

353. Letter Weight, *Sphinx*, rosso antico, on black basalt, Etruria 1783. Hgt. 4".

354. Vase, black basalt, thrown and turned with applied rosso antico decorations, Etruria 1783. Hgt. 4".

355. Candle stick, black basalt, applied acanthus leaves in rosso antico, Etruria 1785. Hgt. 2½".

356. Ink stand, black basalt, applied acanthus leaves and stars in rosso antico, Etruria 1785. Hgt. 4½".

357. Cream jug, rosso antico, embossed, applied black basalt decoration, Etruria 1798. Hgt. 3".

358. Dish and cover, cane, imitation of a pie made during flour shortage in England, Etruria 1793. Length 9½".

359. Bough pot, rosso antico, engine turned basket pattern, applied black basalt decorations, Etruria 1783. Hgt. 7½".

360. Tea pot, cane, engine turned, oval shape, lion knob, Etruria 1798. Hgt. 4".

360a. Tea pot, drab, applied blue ornaments, glazed interior, Etruria 1830. Hgt. 4".

361. Flower pot, rosso antico inlaid with cream color, Etruria 1783. Hgt. 4½".

362. Beer mug, cane, white glaze interior, *Cupids Returning from the Chase*, silver rim, Etruria 1795. Hgt. 4".

363. Vase, rosso antico No. 439 shape, applied black basalt *Gods and Goddesses*, Etruria 1785. Hgt. 15".

364. Pie crust dish, cane, applied white decorations, made to imitate pie crust, Etruria 1795. Hgt. 4½".

365. Game pie dish, cane, made in imitation of pie crust during flour shortage in England, embossed game and grape design on side, rabbit knob, Etruria 1815. Hgt. 4½".

366. Pot, cane, applied black basalt ornaments, interchangeable top for potpourri or bough pot, Etruria 1795. Hgt. 12".

MARBLED WARE

367. Vase, marbled ware, *Mosaic design*, thrown and turned, Etruria 1798. Hgt. 11".

369. Vase, marbled ware, black basalt plinth, porphyry, applied cream color medallion of *Esculatius and Youth*, mask terminal handles, Etruria 1772. Hgt. 12½".

370. Vase, marbled ware, unglazed porphyry, applied white wreath decoration, mask terminal handles, Etruria 1772. Hgt. 4½".

370a. Vase, marbled, applied white festoons, Etruria 1778. Hgt. 10".

371. Vase, marbled ware, porphyry, thrown and turned, applied drapery festoons

and rings, black basalt plinth, Etruria 1772. Hgt. 14½".

372. Bough pot, marbled ware, porphyry, green sprinkled with cream color, applied husk festoons, Etruria 1783. Hgt. 11".

373. Vase, marbled ware, chocolate body with inlays of cream color, pressed and polished, black basalt plinth, Etruria 1775. Hgt. 8½".

374. Bough pot, marbled ware, green with applied white festoons and acanthus leaves, semi-circular, Etruria 1785. Hgt. 5".

375. Candle stick, agate, brown and white, Etruria 1770. Hgt. 5¼".

375a. Vase, marbled ware, black basalt foot and plinth, Etruria 1778. Hgt. 6¼".

376. Vase, marbled ware, inlaid colors, flutes, scroll handles, Etruria 1785. Hgt. 8".

376a. Vase, marbled ware, inlaid with white, applied masks and festoons, Etruria 1778. Hgt. 7".

377. Trial for standardization of marbling, Etruria 1772. Hgt. 3".

377a. Nineteen cut and polished stones and one test piece used as patterns to achieve marbling effects, Etruria Circa 1775.

377b. Ring stand. Prepared clay taken from Whieldon factory site and turned into the form of a ring stand to show the actual grain of colored clays used by Whieldon and Wedgwood in the making of early marbled ware. Also bit of unglazed clay used to make ring stand. Whieldon-Wedgwood 1769. Hgt. 3".

378. Test square for marbling, Etruria Circa 1775. Width 4¾".

379. Vase, marbled ware, sprinkled porphyry, satyr handles in cream colour, Shape No. 1 in original jasper shape book, Etruria 1772. Hgt. 16".

380. Vase, marbled ware, applied festoons, Etruria 1785. Hgt. 7".

381. Flower pot and stand, marbled ware,

blacked interior, Etruria 1774. Hgt. 5″.

382. Vase and cover, agate, cupid finial, black basalt plinth, Etruria 1776. Hgt. 8½″.

383. Vase, marbled ware, porphyry, applied medallion and masks in cream colour, black basalt plinth, Etruria 1773. Hgt. 11″.

384. Vase, marbled ware, thrown and turned, applied handles and leaf festoons, Etruria 1774. Hgt. 8″.

384a. Strip mold for handle used for catalogue no. 384, dated 1768, used at Burslem and still in use today.

385. Vase, agate, pressed, mask terminal handles, black basalt foot, Etruria 1775. Hgt. 7½″.

386. Vase, marbled ware, porphyry, black basalt plinth, scroll handles, Etruria 1773. Hgt. 8½″.

19TH AND 20TH CENTURIES

387. Two plates, Queen's Ware, *Cupids*,
& yellow, blue and sepia, painted by
387a. Emile Lessore, Etruria 1860. Dia. 10″.

388. Two plates, Queen's Ware, yellow, blue
& and sepia, painted by Emile Lessore,
389. Etruria 1866. Dia. 10″.

390. Vase, Queen's Ware, domestic scenes, multicolor, painted by Emile Lessore, Etruria 1868. Hgt. 12½″.

391. Sugar bowl and cover, Queen's Ware, photographic print of boating view, Etruria 1878. Hgt. 4½″.

392. Flower pot, majolica, green and black marbled design, thrown and turned with key runner border, Etruria 1863. Hgt. 4″.

393. Comport, Queen's Ware, inlaid with colored clays, made by T. Mellor, Etruria 1885. Hgt. 3″.

394. Vase and Cover on pedestal, Queen's Ware, inlaid with colored clays, made by T. Mellor, Etruria 1885. Hgt. 15″.

395. Vase, bone china, powder blue, gold dragon, Etruria 1916. Hgt. 14″.

396. Plate, bone china, blue border, gilt decoration, crest in center, Etruria 1895. Dia. 10″.

397. Plate, bone china, blue print, Etruria 1812. Dia. 8″.

398. Soup plate, bone china, White House service made for Theodore Roosevelt, decorated in gold with the seal of the *United States* by Herbert Chollerton, Etruria 1912. Dia. 10″.

399. Sauce tureen, bone china, White House service made for Theodore Roosevelt, decorated in gold with the seal of the United States by Herbert Chollerton, Etruria 1912. Dia. 10″.

400. Plate, bone china, gold decorations, one of 150 Wedgwood plates in the earthquake in San Jose, California, April 18th, 1906. This was the only plate broken although the building collapsed, Etruria 1905. Dia. 10″.

401. Saucer, bone china, blue and gold decoration, Etruria 1812. Dia. 5″.

402. Tea caddy, bone china, powder blue, gold decoration, Etruria 1917. Hgt. 8″.

403. Vase, Queen's Ware, trumpet shape, blue print, Etruria 1850. Hgt. 5″.

404. Covered jar, Queen's Ware, blue print, diaper pattern, ring handles, Etruria 1820. Hgt. 5″.

405. Jug, Queen's Ware, brown print, *Ferrara* pattern engraved by William Brookes, Etruria 1845. Hgt. 6″.

406. Tea cup, trial body, bute shape, blue print, Etruria 1850. Hgt. 2½″.

407. Saucer, Queen's Ware, trial for color in underglaze blue transfer, Etruria 1846. Dia. 5″.

408. Commemorative plate, Brooklyn Bridge, Queen's Ware, blue print made in commemoration of the Tercentenary of Long Island 1636-1936, taken from lithograph by Joseph Pennell, vignettes on border illustrating important Long Island views.

409. Oval dish, Queen's Ware, two color print, printed in blue with black registered over the blue, decorated by

Toft and Austin, Etruria 1856. Length 12″.

410. Plate, Queen's Ware, blue print, Etruria 1850. Dia. 10″.

411. Plate, Queen's Ware, blue print, Etruria 1859. Dia. 10″.

412. Plate, Queen's Ware, blue print, Etruria 1840. Dia. 10″.

414. Lattice basket, Queen's Ware, Etruria 1920. Length 10″.

416. Plate, Queen's Ware, blue print, Etruria 1853. Dia. 8″.

417. Plate, Queen's Ware, blue print, Etruria 1857. Dia. 8″.

418. Covered vegetable dish, bone china, *Sylvia* pattern, designed by Paul Follot, Etruria 1922. Length 9½″.

419. Coffee cup and saucer, bone china, *Sylvia* pattern, designed by Paul Follot, Etruria 1922. Hgt. 2½″.

420. Tea cup and saucer, bone china, *Sylvia* pattern, designed by Paul Follot, Etruria 1922. Hgt. 2½″.

421. Tea service, Queen's Ware, red print, inscribed with quotations on base, Etruria 1878. Teapot 6″ high. ·

422. Plate, bone china, blue groundlay, raised gold and enamel decoration, Etruria 1879.

423. Plate, bone china, *Royal* shape, yellow groundlay with black border, gold decoration, Etruria 1894. Dia. 9″.

424. Plate, bone china, *Gadroon* shape, red groundlay, gold and enamel decoration, Etruria 1900. Dia. 10″.

427. Jug, Queen's Ware, *Moonlight* lustre, Etruria 1806. Hgt. 5″.

428. Compotier, Queen's Ware, *Moonlight* lustre, shell shape, Etruria 1806. Dia. 8″.

429. Cup and saucer, rosso antico body with steel lustre, Etruria 1809. Hgt. 3″.

430. Bust, Parian, *Venus*, Etruria 1850. Hgt. 15″.

431. Figure, Parian, *Ariadne*, Etruria 1850. Hgt. 12″.

432. Vase, Queen's Ware, *Seven Ages of Man* by Walter Crane, mulberry and yellow, Etruria 1867. Hgt. 6″.

433. Candlestick, Queen's Ware, majolica, blue, green, yellow and red, *Dolphin* originally designed by Josiah Wedgwood, Etruria 1860. Hgt. 10″.

433a. Coffee Pot, Rockingham ware, Etruria 1865. Hgt. 8″.

437. Candlestick, cane, applied green and lilac ornaments, smear glaze, Etruria 1830. Hgt. 2″.

438. Vase, cane, applied blue ornaments, glazed interior, Etruria 1830. Hgt. 4″.

439. Coffee biggin, self-colored Queen's Ware, drab, no. 43 shape, forerunner of modern drip coffee pot, Etruria 1850. Hgt. 8″.

440. Broth bowl and cover, self-colored Queen's Ware, drab with robin's egg blue lining, Etruria 1840. Hgt. 3½″.

441. Jug, self-colored Queen's Ware, drab, embossed leaf pattern, Etruria 1840. Hgt. 5″.

442. Jug, self-colored Queen's Ware, drab, monogram "J.P." and gold band, Etruria 1840. Hgt. 4″.

443. Salt pot, self-colored Queen's Ware, drab, engine turned flutes, smear glaze exterior, clear glaze interior, Etruria 1840. Hgt. 1″.

444. Tea cup and saucer, self-colored Queen's Ware, drab, red, blue and green, washed robin's egg blue interior, *Groups* pattern, designed in 1819, Etruria 1840. Hgt. 3″.

445. Mug, self-colored Queen's Ware, Cane, embossed oak design, Etruria 1815. Hgt. 3″.

PERSISTENT PATTERNS

446. Plate, bone china, Lincoln shape, *Charnwood* pattern taken from catalogue no. 447, persistent pattern, red, green, yellow and brown, engraved by Richard Moreton, Barlaston 1945. Dia. 10″.

447. Plate, original blue print of *Charnwood* pattern from Josiah Wedgwood's private collection, 1790. Dia. 10″.

448. Plate, Queen's Ware, original *Napoleon*

Ivy plate, ordered by the British Government for Napoleon when he was exiled to St. Helena, green and brown, Etruria 1815. Dia. 10″.

449. Plate, Queen's Ware, *Napoleon Ivy* design, persistent pattern, from catalogue no. 448, green and brown, Barlaston 1947. Dia. 10″.

450. Original wax model of arabesque border later called *Patrician,* a persistent pattern, Etruria 1775. Dia. 5″.

451. Tea pot, stoneware, smear glaze, adaptation of *Patrician* motif, no. 66 in original shape book, persistent pattern, Etruria 1830. Hgt. 3″.

452. Plate, Queen's Ware, *Barley* pattern, yellow and green, from design in early pattern book, Barlaston 1947. Dia. 10″.

453. Plate, Queen's Ware, *Feather* border, gold and red, from design in early pattern book, persistent pattern, Barlaston 1940. Dia. 10″.

455. Biscuit model, custard cup, *Fir Cone,* a persistent pattern, Etruria 1790. Hgt. 3½″.

456. Custard cup, green glaze, *Fir Cone,* a persistent pattern, made from model catalogue no. 455, Etruria 1860. Hgt. 3″.

457. Custard cup, Queen's Ware, *Fir Cone,* a persistent pattern, made from catalogue no. 455, Etruria 1860. Hgt. 2½″.

458. Biscuit model, *Hunt Jug,* a persistent pattern, Etruria 1800. Hgt. 5″.

460. Salesman's Catalogue showing origin of persistent patterns, Etruria, 1810.

461. Plate, Queen's Ware, *Eastern Flowers,* as first produced in 1845, overglaze enamel colors and lustre, Etruria 1845. Dia. 10″.

461a. Plate, Queen's Ware, *Eastern Flowers,* persistent pattern engraved 1845, reintroduced 1945 in underglaze decoration, brown, yellow, pink and green, Barlaston 1947. Dia. 10″.

462. Plate, Queen's Ware, Queen's shape, original plate from the first service made for Catherine the Great of Russia, *Husk* design, maroon, a persistent pattern, Etruria 1774. Dia. 10″.

462a. Plate, Queen's Ware, Queen's shape, *Husk* design, maroon, a persistent pattern from catalogue no. 462, Barlaston 1947. Dia. 10″.

465. Wall bracket, Queen's Ware, *Nautilus shape, Moonlight lustre,* Etruria 1810. Hgt. 6″.

466. Dessert plate, Queen's Ware, *Nautilus shape, Moonlight Lustre,* Etruria 1808. Dia. 8″.

467. Biscuit model, dessert plate, *Nautilus shape,* designed by Josiah Wedgwood, Etruria 1796. Dia. 8″.

469. Teapot, bone china, *Hackwood Vine,* white, embossed vine, gold outline, persistent pattern, designed by William Hackwood, Etruria 1812. Hgt. 5″.

475. Candlestick, Cinquencento, Queen's Ware, Etruria 1930. Hgt. 11″.

479. Basket, Queen's Ware, Gothic shape, pierced border, Etruria 1850. Hgt. 6″.

480. Butter dish and cover, Queen's Ware, boat shape, Etruria 1783. Hgt. 3″.

481. Wine funnel, Queen's Ware, lotus shape, Etruria 1850. Hgt. 8″.

482. Tea kettle, Queen's Ware, bow handle, vine knob, Etruria 1850. Hgt. 10″.

484. Teapot, Queen's Ware, shape 146, Living Tradition, designed by Josiah Wedgwood and still made today, Barlaston, 1947. Hgt. 5″.

485. Coffee pot, Queen's Ware, shape 129, Living Tradition, designed by Josiah Wedgwood and still made today, Barlaston 1947. Hgt. 8½″.

486. Plate, Queen's Ware, *Concave shape,* Living Tradition, designed by Josiah Wedgwood and still made today, Barlaston 1947. Dia. 10″.

487. Tea cup and saucer, Queen's Ware, *Pear shape,* Living Tradition, designed by Josiah Wedgwood, still made today, Barlaston 1947. Hgt. 3½″.

488. Sauceboat, Queen's Ware, designed by Josiah Wedgwood, still made today, Barlaston 1947. Hgt. 4″.

489. Circular plaque, Queen's Ware, *Barlaston Hall*, painted in purple lustre, designed by Alfred Powell, Barlaston 1942. Dia. 24".

490. Circular plaque, Queen's Ware, *Sailing Ships*, painted in mat platinum, moonstone and silver, designed by Alfred Powell, Barlaston 1940. Dia. 16".

491. Circular plaque, Queen's Ware, *White Stag*, underglaze blue, gray and green, designed by Alfred Powell, Etruria 1938. Dia. 16".

492. Circular plaque, Queen's Ware, white with silver lustre decoration, designed by Alfred Powell, Etruria 1930. Dia. 22".

493. *Sea Lion*, self-colored body, Celadon, modeled by John Skeaping, Etruria 1930. Hgt. 9".

494. *Lying Duiker*, self-colored body, cane, modeled by John Skeaping, Etruria 1930. Hgt. 5".

495. Plate, self-colored body, *Wintergreen*, celadon center, white rim, Etruria 1936. Dia. 10".

496. Plate, Queen's Ware, celadon, *Richborough*, designed by Edward Overton-Jones, Etruria 1939. Dia. 8".

497. Teapot, self-colored body, *Harvest Moon*, shape 146, Etruria 1936. Hgt. 5".

498. Covered jug, self-colored body, *Summer Sky*, blue, shape 129, Etruria 1936. Hgt. 5½".

499. Plate, Queen's Ware, *Crowned Seal*, purple, yellow and brown, designed by Carol Janeway, Barlaston 1948. Dia. 10".

500. Plate, Queen's Ware, *Quilting Bird*, green and yellow, designed by Carol Janeway, Barlaston 1948. Dia. 10".

501. Bowl, new shapes and glazes developed by Norman Wilson, Adventurine glaze interior, black mat glaze exterior, Barlaston 1946. Dia. 6½".

502. Bowl, new shapes and glazes developed by Norman Wilson, canary yellow interior, black mat exterior, Barlaston 1946. Dia. 8¾".

503. Plate, bone china, *Laurentia*, multicolor designed by Edward Overton-Jones; this design inspired by a brocade worn by Martha Washington, Etruria 1939. Dia. 10".

504. Cup and saucer, *Coronation*, ruby groundlay, feather design in mat platinum, designed by Star Wedgwood, Etruria 1936. Hgt. 3".

505. Cream soups and stand, bone china, *Pimpernel*, pink groundlay gray flowers, designed by Victor Skellern, Barlaston 1947. Dia. 6½".

506. Plate, bone china, *Greyfriars*, gray groundlay rim, floral pattern in gray and pink, designed by Victor Skellern, Barlaston 1947. Dia. 10".

507. Dessert plate, celadon, *Forest Folk*, designed by Victor Skellern, Etruria 1934. Dia. 8".

508. Plate, Queen's Ware, Catherine shape, *Seasons*, sepia, designed by Victor Skellern, Etruria 1935. Dia. 8".

509. Bowl, Queen's Ware, *Quayside*, moonstone, glaze, grayish green, painted, designed by Victor Skellern, Barlaston 1946. Dia. 9½".

510. Compotier, bone china, ruby groundlay, gold shells, designed by Victor Skellern, Etruria 1937. Dia. 9".

511. Two dessert plates, bone china, pink textured bands, painted with gold, designed by Victor Skellern, Etruria 1939. Dia. 8".

512. Coffee set, bone china, *Persian Pony*, ruby groundlay, black motif, designed by Victor Skellern, Etruria 1936. Pot hgt. 8¼".

513. Figure, *Beatrice*, terra cotta, modeled by Arnold Machin, Barlaston 1944. Hgt. 2' 6".

515. Figure, *Penelope*, Queen's Ware, slip decoration, modeled by Arnold Machin, Barlaston 1944. Hgt. 11".

516. Figure, *Bridal Group*, Queen's Ware,

115

slip decoration, modeled by Arnold Machin, Barlaston 1941. Hgt. 10½″.

517. Head, *Cherub*, terra cotta with Staffordshire salt glaze, modeled by Arnold Machin, Barlaston 1944. Hgt. 5″.

518. Figure, *Taurus*, terra cotta with incised decoration, modeled by Arnold Machin, Barlaston 1945. Hgt. 7″.

519. Bust, *Lucrecia*, terra cotta, modeled by Arnold Machin, Barlaston 1944. Hgt. 1′ 10″.

520. Bust, *Portrait of Susan*, terra cotta, modeled by Arnold Machin, Barlaston 1943. Hgt. 1′ 8″.

521. Bust, *Portrait of Madelaine*, terra cotta, modeled by Arnold Machin, Barlaston 1946. Hgt. 1′ 9″.

522. Teapot, rosso antico, shape 43, Etruria 1939. Hgt. 11″.

524. Bowl, black basalt, thrown and turned, designed by Keith Murray, Etruria 1936. Hgt. 4″.

525. Plate, bone china, *Appledor*, enameled blue border and floral center, designed by Wedgwood Studios, Etruria 1936. Dia. 8″.

526. Vase, two color slip ware, cream and celadon, shape 4215, designed by Keith Murray, Etruria 1938. Hgt. 7″.

527. Vase, two color slip ware, cream and celadon, shape 4220, designed by Keith Murray, Etruria 1938. Hgt. 8″.

528. Jug and mug, Queen's Ware, thrown and turned, Dysart glaze, shape 3810, designed by Keith Murray, Etruria 1933. Jug hgt. 10″.

529. Commemorative mug, made at the opening of Barlaston, Queen's Ware, lithographic print, designed by Eric Ravilious, Barlaston 1940. Hgt. 5″.

530. Bowl, Queen's Ware, *Boat Race*, underglaze black enameled colors designed by Eric Ravilious, Etruria 1938. Dia. 12″.

531. Liverpool jug and beaker, Queen's Ware, *Garden Implements* pattern, printed underglaze black, hand painted pink lustre, designed by Eric Ravilious, Etruria 1937. Jug hgt. 7¾″.

532. Plate, Queen's Ware, *Persephone* pattern, printed in underglaze black, painted bands, blue center, designed by Eric Ravilious, Etruria 1937. Dia. 10″.

533. Plate, Queen's Ware, *Garden* pattern, printed underglaze black, band and center enameled yellow, designed by Eric Ravilious, Etruria 1938. Dia. 10″.

534. Coffee set, bone china, ruby groundlay, white and gold sgraffito motif, designed by Millicent Taplin, Etruria 1939. Hgt. 8¼″.

535. Cup and saucer, bone china, *Whitehall* pattern, powder ruby with gold vine leaf border, Barlaston 1947. Plate dia. 10″.

536. Compotier, self-colored bone china, *Alpine Pink*, Nautilus shape, introduced, Etruria 1936. Pot hgt. 8¼″.

537. Plate, bone china, *Windrush* pattern, turquoise groundlay, handpainted gray leaf motif, designed by Millicent Taplin, Barlaston 1947. Dia. 10″.

538. After-dinner cup and saucer, bone china, *Ulander* pattern, powder turquoise rim with gold edge, Barlaston 1947. Dia. 10″.

539. Bouillon and stand, bone china, *Avon* pattern, white enameled interpretation of Tonquin pattern, Barlaston 1947. Dia. 6½″.

540. Plate, bone china, *Wildflower* pattern, turquoise groundlay, gray floral motif, designed by Victor Skellern, Barlaston 1947. Dia. 10″.

541. Plate, bone china, *Bideford* pattern, enameled floral decoration, designed by Wedgwood Studios, Barlaston 1947. Dia. 10″.

542. After dinner cup and saucer, bone china, *Josephine* pattern, yellow groundlay, gray ivy leaf design as on Napoleon Ivy, Barlaston 1947. Plate dia. 10″.

543. Cream jug, bone china, *Falling Leaves* pattern, hand painted green, gray and silver, designed by Millicent Taplin, Etruria 1930. Hgt. 5″.

544. Triple tray, Queen's Ware, *Bramble,* shell edge, engraved 1862, Barlaston 1947. Dia. 11¼".

545. Square cake plate, Queen's Ware, *Cornflower* pattern, engraved by Sherwin 1860, Barlaston 1947. Width 9".

546. Cover dish, Queen's Ware, *Surrey* pattern, Barlaston 1947, Dia. 8".

547. Plate, cup and saucer, Queen's Ware, *Autumn* pattern, brown and red, designed by Millicent Taplin, Etruria 1938. Plate dia. 10".

548. Sugar and cream, Queen's Ware, *Bramble* pattern, shell edge, Barlaston 1947. Hgt. 4".

549. Hunt jug, Queen's Ware, hunting scene, hound handle, multicolor, Barlaston 1947. Hgt. 8".

550. Oval basket, hand embossed Queen's Ware, *Grape Vine,* lavender on cream color, from original molds made in 1775, Barlaston 1947. Length 13½".

551. Garden pot, hand embossed Queen's Ware, pink on cream color, from original molds made in 1775, Barlaston 1947. Hgt. 5".

552. Vase, hand embossed Queen's Ware, *Grape Vine,* cream on lavender, from original molds made in 1775, Barlaston 1947. Hgt. 10".

553. Plate, hand embossed, Queen's Ware, *Grape Vine,* cream on lavender, from original molds made in 1775, Barlaston 1947. Dia. 10".

554. Cream soup and stand, hand embossed, Queen's Ware, *Grape Vine,* cream color, from original molds made in 1775, Barlaston 1947, Dia. 6¾".

555. Plate, bouillon and stand, Queen's Ware, *Evenlode* pattern, turquoise border with center of wild roses on Corinthian shape, designed by Victor Skellern, Barlaston 1947. Plate Dia. 10".

556. Plate, Queen's Ware, *Morning Glory* pattern, on Patrician shape, designed by Victor Skellern, Barlaston, 1947. Dia. 10".

562. Utility ware, made for use in England during Second World War, undecorated Queen's Ware designed for economy of production as well as to fill the demand for functional dinnerware, Barlaston 1940.

PAINTINGS AND
DOCUMENTARY MATERIAL

563. Portrait, oil, *Josiah Wedgwood, F.R.S.,* by Sir Joshua Reynolds, 1783. Size 30½" x 25½".

564. Portrait, oil, *Mrs. Josiah Wedgwood,* (Sarah, daughter of Richard Wedgwood), by Sir Joshua Reynolds, 1783. Size 30½" x 25½".

565. Portrait, oil, *Mrs. Elizabeth Wedgwood,* (Bessie Allen) wife of Josiah II, three-quarter length, by George Romney, 1790. Size 50½" x 40½".

566. Painting, oil, *View of Etruria* in 1790, by Robert W. Baker, Principal, City of Stoke-on-Trent School of Art, 1948. Size 12' x 20'.

567. Painting, oil, *View of Barlaston* in 1948, by Robert W. Baker, Principal, City of Stoke-on-Trent School of Art, 1948. Size 12' x 20'.

569. Painting, oil, *Wedgwood's Old Mill,* by Vonk, 1814. Size 12" x 9".

570. Painting, oil, *Brickhouse Works,* Burslem, by Vonk, 1814. Size 12" x 9".

571. Painting, oil, *Ivy House Works,* Burslem, artist unknown, 1814. Size 12" x 9".

579. Letter from Josiah Wedgwood to Thomas Bentley with Josiah's statement, "Blessed my stars and Lord North that America is free," March 19, 1778.

580. Acknowledgment from Josiah Wedgwood on receiving the Portland Vase from His Grace the Duke of Portland, 1786.

581. Letter from Josiah Wedgwood to Thomas Bentley mentioning being obliged to lower prices, and that troops were being recalled from American Colonies, March 19, 1779.

582. Indenture in which Gilbert Wedgwood

is mentioned in conveyance of land, 1637.

583. Partnership indenture between Josiah Wedgwood and Thomas Bentley, 1769.

584. Work book of Whieldon-Wedgwood, 1757.

585. Letter of 1886 relating to original Napoleon Ivy plate of 1815.

588. Manuscript of address made by William Ewart Gladstone, Prime Minister of England, at the opening of the Wedgwood Institute at Burslem in 1863.

589. Invoice to Mr. John Flaxman from Josiah Wedgwood Potter to Her Majesty, 1781) signed by Thomas Byerley, 1781.

590. Letter from John Flaxman to Josiah Wedgwood, 1782.

591. Letter from Josiah Wedgwood to Lady Templetown, February 1788.

592. Diary of Thomas Griffiths on his voyage to America, Cherokee Nation, South Carolina, in search of clay, 1767-1768.

593. Two sheets from Josiah Wedgwood's pattern book of 1770.

594. Shape Book of Josiah Wedgwood, 1770.

595. Description of Portland Vase by Josiah Wedgwood, 1790.

596. Autograph of William Hackwood on bill for finishing wax group of infants representing music as a companion to Sir Joshua's *Infant Academy*, 1785.

597. Autograph of Henry Webber, 1786.

598. List of subscribers to the Portland Vase from Thomas Byerley's notebook, 1789.

599. Drawing of figures for the Portland Vase, 1790.

600. Drawing of figures for Portland Vase, 1790.

601. Josiah Wedgwood's original Experiment Book, 1759.

602. Book of Numbers, key to experiments, Circa 1778.

603. Patent for encaustic colors, 1770.

604. Print of John Flaxman, after Jackson, 1827.

605. Account book of Josiah Wedgwood, dating from 1770.

606. Book of Words, Historical Pageant in Commemoration of the Bicentenary of Josiah Wedgwood's Birth, 1730-1930.

607. Plaster model of the Wedgwood Barlaston Estate, Stoke-on-Trent, England, showing present and future development, made by Kenneth McCutchean. Architect for village, Louis de Soissons. Architects for factory, Keith Murray and C. S. White.

608. Clock, oak, 1806. One of the earliest forms of the "Timing On" clock now universally employed in industry. Made by John Whitehurst, Derby, England for Wedgwood. Hgt. 6' 2".

609. *The Combat*, oil, painted on Wedgwood plaque by George Stubbs, circa 1779. Size 20½" x 29". Lent by E. J. Rousuck.

610. Toilet Cabinet, rosewood, Wedgwood jasper plaques, cut steel mounts, English, end of the 18th century. Said to have come from Kensington Palace and to have been owned by Queen Charlotte, wife of George III, for whom Josiah named his Queen's Ware. Height 42", width 18", depth 12". Lent by Metropolitan Museum of Art.

611. Pyrometer found on Whieldon-Wedgwood site, March 1924, believed to be the earliest form of pyrometer from which Josiah Wedgwood developed his perfected model, 1762.

612. Pyrometer brass and test pieces invented by Josiah Wedgwood, 1783.

613. Pyrometer or thermometer developed by Josiah Wedgwood for measuring high degrees of heat "from red hot to the strongest that vessels made of clay can support." For his discoveries in this method of measuring heat, Josiah Wedgwood was elected Fellow of the Royal Society, 1782.